CW01638820

DALE VINE'S OUTDOOR RENO GUIDE

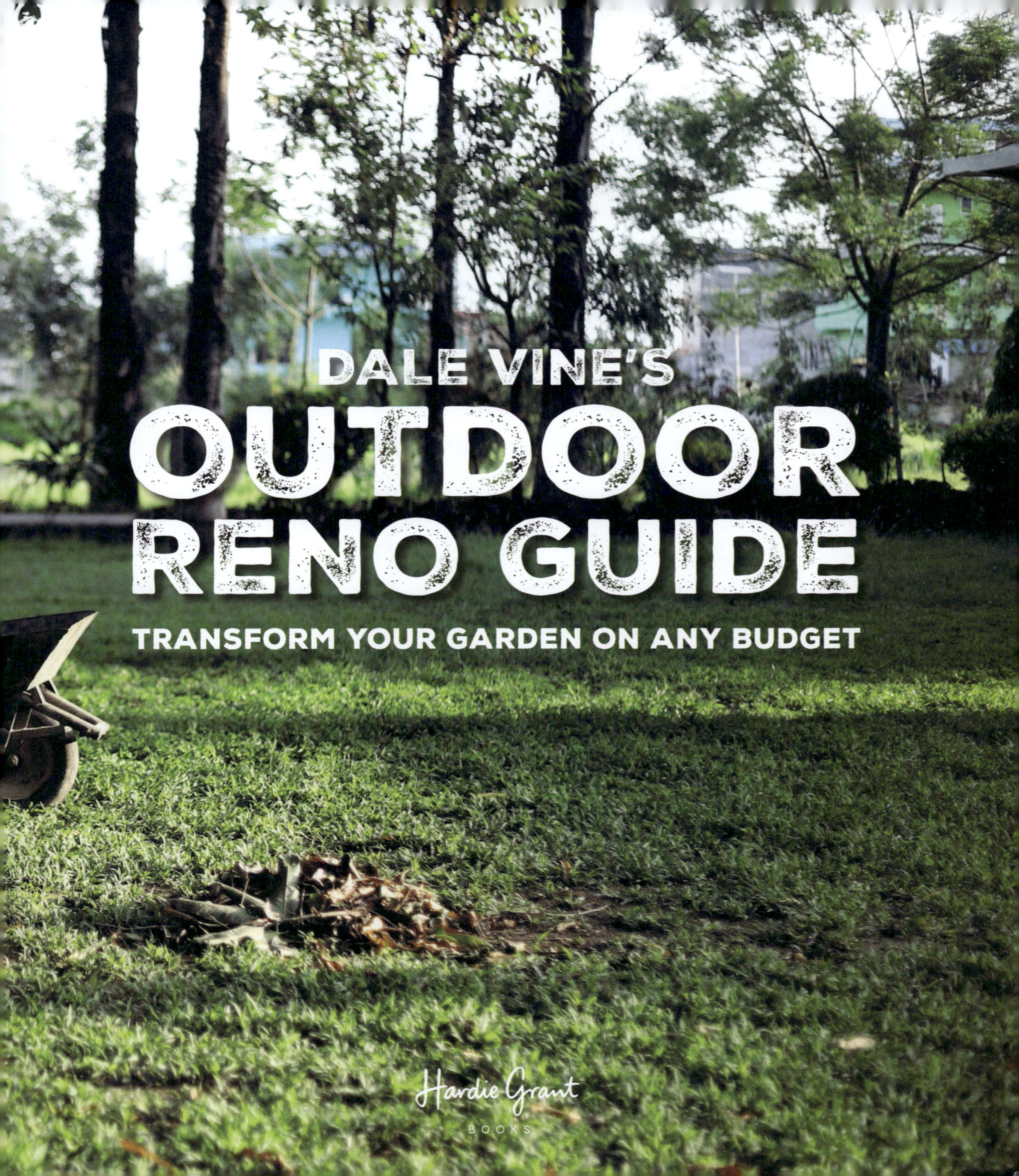

DALE VINE'S

OUTDOOR RENO GUIDE

TRANSFORM YOUR GARDEN ON ANY BUDGET

Hardie Grant
BOOKS

CONTENTS

INTRODUCTION

I feel very fortunate to have been raised with a significant connection to both nature and the land. My father's side of the family were wheat and sheep farmers, and my mother's side avid gardeners who owned a nursery for a while. Nana and grandpa loved plants so much that gardening was almost their weekend sport – one they just happened to play all week long! I was introduced to the art of bonsai at an early age by my grandpa Frank, and still do bonsai to this day. Ask my wife, Sophie. I've got enough bonsai to start my own nursery.

There is a very real sense of calm I get when walking around a nursery, selecting plants for current projects. In my head I'm already grouping them together to plant on site, creating these little ecosystems for my clients to enjoy.

I'm one of those classic blokes who can't sit still for more than a few minutes without feeling like the day is wasting away. On the weekend you'll find me outside creating small jobs for myself, just to get out of the house. It truly is my happy place – and now, with three young kids, I can't wait to pass on to them my passion for getting outside among nature and plants and creating beautiful spaces.

When Sophie and I were looking for our first home, I found my eyes glazing over at the features inside the properties and heading straight outside to see what there was to work with. I feel extremely lucky to love what I do for a living. In fact, I didn't really choose landscaping as a profession; it was more that I was bound to end up being a landscaper, no matter which path I took.

Landscaping is one of the most diverse trades you could possibly come across, since it draws upon all sorts of elements and skills from other trades and melds them all together in a single profession. We find ourselves not just shaping soil and digging in plants, but building, plumbing, installing low-voltage electrical fittings, painting, tiling, bricklaying and much more. It's a multi-skilled trade that basically covers all aspects outside the home, and even some things within it.

Which brings me to why I'm writing this book. There are plenty of high-end landscaping books available, each of which will show you some of the amazing gardens that can be created. They'll pop out at you page after glossy page, making you dream that something similar could be yours. The reality, however, is that for many average homeowners, most of these gardens are far out of reach. So instead, I'd like to show you how to get the most from your outdoor spaces in a way that is completely achievable. I'll give you the heads-up on the factors to consider if you decide to work with a landscaper to streamline the whole process, so you can get maximum effect for your available budget, and with a professional finish.

My aim is to leave you, the reader, equipped with the knowledge to make the process of creating beautiful outdoor spaces as easy as possible, so you can get to that point where you are simply enjoying your garden, now and for years to come. I've thrown in a few simple how-tos in most chapters for anyone who wants to save a bit of money and isn't afraid to get their hands dirty. If that's you, it'll mean you can allocate more money to getting the rest of the job done by a professional if you need to.

After all, everybody should be able to create a garden that is beautiful and practical, and somewhere they enjoy spending their spare time. Your dream garden is achievable, as long as you go about it the right way. This book will help show you how.

So let's get started – I hope you'll have fun dreaming about, planning, designing and, ultimately, enjoying your outdoor space.

DALE

CHAPTER 1

IMAGINING YOUR GARDEN

The vision splendid

Have you ever been in one of those conversations where someone is trying to explain something to you – and no matter how many questions you ask, you just can't work out what they're going on about? Welcome to the world of landscape designers meeting a client for the first time.

You might have an epic vision of how you'd like your garden to look, but we can't dip into your head to see it. So, the first thing you should do – even before you consult a landscape designer – is to begin a 'vision board' or scrapbook. Collecting images of garden elements you like will help you develop a clear vision of your future outdoor space – one that you can then show to a landscape designer, to tradespeople and nursery folk, explaining where you'd like to see different features and what type of plants you prefer.

GET SNAPPING

COMPILE A VISION BOARD

BROWSE

Seeking garden inspiration

These days, there are lots of sources of wonderful images. Social media sites such as Pinterest are a great place to start, because you can file your 'inspo' images in different folders that are easy to access on both your home computer and your smartphone. Many home interior and design magazines devote entire sections to garden and landscape design. If you see something you particularly like, don't just rip the photo out for your scrapbook – find the designer's name and check out their social media pages. Be prepared to go down an Instagram hole, though, as you begin checking out the designers they follow, and the ones they follow, and so on.

Once you've begun visualising your future garden, you'll also start noticing other people's gardens when you're walking around your neighbourhood. Snap them with your phone and add them to your inspiration guide. On the off-chance someone asks you why you're taking photos, simply tell them you love their garden and you'd like to use it for inspiration. A little flattery goes a long way.

As a landscape designer, I'd say about nine out of ten clients find it hard to answer the simplest of questions about style, space and plantings if they haven't already sat down, gathered their images and mapped out – in their heads, at least – how their ideas are going to work in the space they have.

I can't tell you how much easier it makes my job when a client can show me what they love. Give me a photograph of an entertaining area, show me an example of the paver you'd like to use, tell me where you envisage it sitting in your own garden and I can work with that. Try to explain it to me with no visuals and it all gets a little bit interpretative.

And while images showing the overall big picture are great, don't forget about the little things either. Start gathering pictures of all the elements you like when it comes to plants, structures, building materials (whether that's timber decking, tiles or outdoor pavers), colour palettes and outdoor furniture. These will all make planning your outdoor spaces so much easier. If you are working with a landscape designer, rest assured, we don't expect you to know the names of everything – especially plants – but a picture gives us an indication of the type of look and style you're after.

Choosing a style to suit your lifestyle

One of the great things about landscape design is that you don't necessarily have to match the facade of your home to the style of your garden. You can, of course, if that's the way you want to go. For example, if you live in a Victorian-style terrace and would prefer a traditional garden pairing, or you have a modernist home and are after a more contemporary garden style to suit. Just take a look around, find other homes built in a similar era to see what looks good, and use that for landscape inspiration.

By far, though, you'll find a 'modern' or contemporary garden design is the most popular these days, with clean lines introducing geometric forms, while also incorporating a lot of hard surfaces in the form of natural stones, timber and even steel. Timber is crucial in modern design; it provides a feeling of warmth. Because planting is minimalised in this style, plant selection is even more vital to create a softening effect. This is particularly true in areas set aside for family use – whether that's simply a space to sit and enjoy the sunshine, or somewhere for the kids to play.

This style of garden continues to evolve with emerging lifestyle trends. These days, the average homeowner has to work long

CLEAN, MODERN, MINIMALIST

CONSIDER HOW OFTEN YOU
WILL ACTUALLY USE A HIGH-
END ENTERTAINING AREA

hours, and often their home is their ultimate expense. This means people frequently find themselves with less time and energy to socialise when they do have time off, particularly given the number of hours we spend glued to our screens and phones.

While many busy people may be entertaining less at home, in high-end design the request for large entertaining areas with decks, outdoor rooms and fire pits is still quite prominent. This is often because a large chunk of money was put aside during a renovation to ensure these elements can be added. The reality, however, is that for the average homeowner, these areas cost significantly more money to create and maintain relative to how much use they'll actually get once completed.

Before making any hard and fast decisions about how much money you're going to spend, and on what features, take some time to consider your overall needs and stage of life.

THE YOUNG PROFESSIONAL

When it comes to a garden or landscape design, many young professionals with busy working lives are looking for something neat, tidy and low maintenance. After all, if you fall into this category, would you rather be mowing the lawn on Saturday morning or hang out with friends having brunch at a cafe? Exactly. This means you'll fare best implementing simple planting schemes with species that don't require constant trimming, fertilising and other maintenance, with either synthetic turf or paved areas filling the gaps in between.

Rather than seeing the value in quality landscaping, many young professionals are more likely to value the fit-out and furnishings inside their homes, preferring to spend their money on expensive benchtops, tiles, blinds, designer furniture and large televisions and entertainment systems.

SYNTHETIC TURF

THE YOUNG FAMILY

A lovely flat patch of lawn is something many parents with a young family consider a must-have. Perfect for a kids' play area, the lawn can become a true multi-use area for trampolines, swing sets, inflatable pools, cubby houses and the other fun things that can keep kids entertained for hours. Plus, there's often also a family dog to take into account – and we all know how tough they can be on a garden. A hardy lawn species, such as kikuyu, is ideal for a family situation. Compared with other species, I find it bounces back more quickly from heavy foot traffic, whether that's from kids, dogs or both. And during the dormant cooler months, it won't get as patchy and

KIKUYU GRASS

A SIMPLE PATCH OF
LAWN IS A MUST-HAVE
FOR MANY YOUNG
FAMILIES

MOWING: A WEEKEND
FAMILY RITUAL

A PLACE FOR YOUNG ADULTS
TO HANG OUT

ravaged by wear and tear as grass species such as buffalo or tall fescue.

Some fruit trees for the kids to learn about self-sufficiency also never go astray. Fruit trees are family friendly – they grow big enough to avoid being damaged and destroyed by pets, provide greenery for the garden and supply you with beautiful home-grown produce.

Often, the task of tending to a lawn can become a family affair on the weekend, with Dad watching the kids play as he mows. When the kids get a bit older, this task can then be passed on to them as they start to take on more household chores to earn a bit of pocket money. It's funny how the lawn can involve the whole family in more ways than just play.

THE FAMILY WITH HIGH SCHOOL OR UNI STUDENTS

Fast forward a decade or so and the young family has grown up in their home. The kids are now completing high school, or are even studying at university (but still live at home to save on rent, food and other essential living expenses). These homes are the most likely to feature a pool and outdoor entertaining areas, so parents can provide a place for their young adults to have friends over and enjoy themselves without worrying where they are, or just to get them away from study and computer screens for a well-earned break.

These gardens are all about purpose of use, and most often include built-in barbecue areas, undercover outdoor entertaining spaces with tables and seating for gatherings, and lighting for social night-time use. Because all these hard-surfaced entertaining areas can be expensive to construct, often the sacrifice in budget is made on the plantings, meaning smaller stock sizes are used initially and can take some years to mature.

THE DOWNSIZERS

Then there are the downsizers – the older couples who, once their children have grown up and left the family home, are left with a place that's far too big for their current needs. This often means the large family home gets sold, and they buy or build something smaller that better suits their pending retirement lifestyle. This can go one of two ways when it comes to the garden design.

The first option is very similar to the low-maintenance approach favoured by young professionals. However, the empty-nester may have a bigger budget for a few nice features, such as outdoor furnishings, a built-in barbecue area or a pergola. Their

garden design might also incorporate some mature-sized plants, which offer instant effect – unlike smaller plants that take years to establish. This is a popular approach for retirees who wish to live out their later years in their new home but also know they'll be away for longer periods as they travel and explore the world.

The second scenario is the non-travelling older couple or person, who enjoys tending their garden as a means of leisure. Their preferred garden designs often include larger areas of garden beds, with more exotic plantings of annuals and perennials to create seasonal interest. Of course, these types of gardens and plantings require far more hands-on maintenance and are best reserved for the keen gardener. That was the case with my grandparents: an automated watering system was never required as my grandpa would happily stand out in the garden with a hose from 6 am every morning.

MATURE-SIZED PLANTS
OFFER INSTANT EFFECT

HOW DOES YOUR GARDEN GROW?

When sketching out your dream garden, remember to base it around your needs and lifestyle, taking into account how much time you'll have to maintain it and which features you'll get the most use and enjoyment from. Here are the main elements of different popular garden styles, to help you on your way.

FAMILY FRIENDLY

- Lawn areas
- Open play spaces
- Shade
- Cubby house and other play equipment
- Outdoor entertaining and leisure

CONTEMPORARY

- Clean lines
- Stand-out feature plants, such as maples, silver birch and buxus spheres
- Sleek outdoor areas
- Modern hard materials

COTTAGE GARDEN

- Mixed plantings of flowers and grasses with depth, layering and interest, such as wisteria, delphiniums and daisies
- Winding paths to different areas of the garden to create interest
- Whimsical

LOW MAINTENANCE

- Synthetic lawn or hard surfaces
- Succulents such as agave and sedum, or natives such as xanthorrhoea species
- Small need for hands-on hours: minimal weeding, watering and trimming requirements

VEGIE-PATCH STYLE

- Raised or defined garden beds or areas for herbs and productive crops such as heirloom tomatoes, beans, corn, rhubarb, spinach and lettuce
- Paths made from recycled materials
- Compost heap, worm farm
- Organic focus

NATIVE GARDEN

- Natural look
- Plantings of native species, including insect- and fauna-attracting plants such as correa, westringia, grevillea, hakea and leptospermum
- Use of natural stone
- Organic mulch
- Low water needs
- Generally low maintenance

ENGLISH-STYLE GARDEN

- Symmetry
- Formal plantings, such as buxus, roses and lavender
- Paths of paved patterns, or gravel and grass paths
- Defined borders, using plants such as buxus, roses, lavender, hydrangea and salvia

WHAT COULD GO WRONG?

While you might be inspired to attempt all the landscaping work yourself, you could end up with an area that doesn't work for its purpose if you don't properly think all the elements and required steps through. You could also end up jamming too much into a space that can't accommodate so many elements. A classic example is someone who buys a new plant or feature they like the look of every time they go to the nursery, without thinking of where – or even *if* – it fits into their garden.

If you decide to tackle elements like paving yourself, you could spend many hours – even days – working on something that has to be fixed by a professional later on, and that will end up costing far more than you'd anticipated. I know I wouldn't attempt to replace engine parts in my car, since I don't know anything about it, and if I tried, it would likely cost me more money to fix what I'd messed up. It's the same with garden design and landscaping: you may find that investing in a little professional guidance can go a long way.

CHAPTER 2

DESIGNING FOR LIFE

Little people and furry friends

We've already touched on the importance of designing your garden based on the needs of the people who are actually going to be using the space.

As we have seen, for many homeowners – from young professionals to retired downsizers – the amount of time they have to enjoy their space (and maintain it) will influence their decisions when it comes to garden design. But if you have kids and pets – or are contemplating adding them to your family – there are definitely extra considerations to take into account.

Yes, it's one thing to create a magnificently lush garden full of gorgeous plants, trickling waterfalls and interesting sculptures, but it's quite another to see them being destroyed by kids kicking balls into them and dogs jumping and peeing all over them.

DOGS LOVE TO DIG!

BIGGER PLANTS ARE MORE CANINE-PROOF

WATERING SYSTEMS CAN BE POTENTIAL CHEW TOYS

Dogs and design

As much as we love our canine friends, there's the old saying that dogs and beautiful gardens don't really go together. That's not entirely true, the two can co-exist – if you devise a few strategies to deter curious, bored or playful dogs from destroying elements of a garden.

TURF WARS

For outdoor spaces that are home to larger dogs, synthetic turf may be a better option than real grass. Dogs often create their own high-traffic areas, by running along fence lines for instance. A real lawn will wear down, die back and won't bounce back well – especially during winter months when the grass becomes dormant. Of course, no lawn will cope if your pooch enjoys digging holes.

WATER WORKS

For canines, watering systems can be another doggy treat. Poly pipes, spiked drippers, sprinklers or shrubblers at the base of plants can be favourite chew toys. Hence, in a yard you'll share with your dog, selecting hardier plant species that don't require a permanent watering system is often the way to go.

GO FOR BIG

In areas of the yard where Rover is free to roam, the extra expense of opting for more mature trees or plants could prove worthwhile. They are more likely to survive interest from your canine friend, compared to smaller plants that can be trampled, chewed or dug up.

FENCE FIDO IN

In a larger outdoor space, you could also consider using clever fencing to create separate garden zones. This will leave areas where your pooch can play, and others where you can install some nice outdoor furniture, a vegie patch or garden beds with more delicate plantings.

A WEE TRICK

You might also want to think about adding an element or two that will let your dog mark out its space well away from your barbecue or good outdoor furniture. A couple of large, sculptural stones or pieces of driftwood can give them a place to pee, and save anything you hold dear from regular canine spraying.

CREATING A DOG-PROOF FENCE

You might be lucky enough to move into a house that already has a high fence around it. But if you don't, you'll need to install one well before your dog moves in. Never underestimate the canine potential to escape!

Tall fences – at least 1.2 metres high for a small dog, and up to 1.8 metres for large dogs – will stop them jumping over into a neighbour's yard or out onto the street. However, you also might need to consider the fact that great diggers will try to escape by burrowing their way underneath a fence!

Steel fences, such as Colorbond, are virtually impenetrable. Solid timber fences are also a good option, but you'll need to ensure the boards are double nailed or screwed at the bottom to stop inquisitive dogs from pushing their way out.

If your dog is one who likes to break free, consider having a concrete footing, about 30 centimetres deep, running along the full length of the fence, so they can't dig a trench beneath it and slither out to the other side.

Any sort of tall gate should also have its latch up high – escape-artist dogs can soon learn to operate latches at waist height. (A high latch can come in handy for child safety, too.)

Some people install picket-style fences, but dogs can get their paws stuck between them when they try to jump out. Other dogs will use any sort of railing as a type of ladder.

If your dog has been in the family for a while, you might know the likelihood of an escape, but if you're in the preparation stages of getting one, it's important to consider all your fencing options – it's better to be safe than sorry.

Remember, too, that dog-proof fences are also likely to keep kids in ...

CAT

IT'S POISONOUS! PLANTS THAT ARE TOXIC TO DOGS

Sometimes we forget that plants aren't just beautiful – some are actually poisonous to animals. Since dogs like to chew things, make sure you don't plant any of the following species in your yard, or you may end up with a seriously sick pet – or worse.

These are definitely plants to avoid if you have a dog:

- Tulips, daffodils and autumn crocus, especially the bulbs
- Sago palms, especially the nuts
- Oleander
- Cyclamen varieties
- Azaleas
- Amaryllis

It's also worth remembering that peace lilies – one of the most popular, easy-care houseplants – are also toxic to dogs and cats.

TULIPS
DAFFODILS
AUTUMN CROCUS
SAGO PALMS
OLEANDER
CYCLAMEN
AZALEAS
AMARYLLIS

Creating family-friendly gardens

Not so long ago, family homes – in Australia at least – were renowned for being built on large blocks of land, with lots of space to stretch out in the backyard, meaning children of growing families had plenty of areas to run, dig, hide, build and play. Now, with space dwindling (particularly in cities and new suburban areas where houses are increasingly being built on smaller blocks), it becomes even more important to think of how to best use the available space for activities incorporating children's play. Here's how to design with kids in mind.

SPACE AGE

Most kids need some form of open space to run, spin, jump and do all the sorts of energetic crazy things they love to do – whether it's on lawn or areas of decking or paving (although these aren't as nice and soft and springy underfoot as real grass). Any of these spaces can be treated like a blank canvas, allowing for an ever-changing play environment with multiple uses, and they can be home to different kinds of equipment such as trampolines, portable slides, climbing equipment, toys and inflatable pools.

KEEP 'EM CURIOUS

It's a really great idea to create features or areas in backyards that will engage young minds. Kids' imaginations can turn a small corner area with a group planting of three or four silver birch trees into a magical forest; a retaining wall or garden edge built with large rocks becomes the tallest mountain in the world; and a cubby house can offer a whole universe of make-believe and fun. It doesn't take much, but with a few carefully selected materials and planned areas, you can still provide a space that will allow growing children to invent, play and enjoy.

SAFETY FIRST!

If children's play is a major focus in a backyard design, safety must *always* be taken into consideration. It's important to know your children will be safe as they explore their environment, and although they should be supervised at all times, incorporating some commonsense safety elements will give you a bit more peace of mind. Eliminating hazards such as sharp corners, brackets hanging off walls at eye height, steep areas, ponds and other water hazards, as well as avoiding thorny or skin-irritating plants are just some of the things you can do.

LANDSCAPING A RENTAL PROPERTY

If you happen to have an investment property and would like it to yield a good rental return, an appealing garden can be a highly desirable feature. A garden that's attractive and inviting will be a major drawcard for some renters – but you don't want to make a rod for your own back by creating a garden that is too high maintenance. Some tenants will be happy to water a few plants, others might mow a small bit of turf, and if you're lucky, you might score a renter who really loves spending time in the garden and trims shrubs and even adds flowers to it. You shouldn't count on it though.

Here are a few landscaping tricks that can help add value to a rental home.

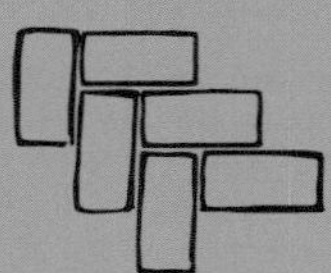

PAVED AREAS

HARDY NATIVE PLANTS

WILD GRASSES

SYNTHETIC TURFS

- **PAVED AREAS** where someone can set up a small table – either undercover or in the shade of a tree – are great to relax in, easy to care for and offer something a little extra.

- **HARDY NATIVE PLANTS** that don't require much water or maintenance are also an excellent addition to a rental garden. If you are stuck for ideas, check out your local nursery and see what they recommend.

- **WILD GRASSES** add visual interest, texture and different heights to the landscaping and, again, don't need much care. Good options include coast tussock grass (*Poa poiformis*), Spiny-headed rush (*Lomandra longifolia*), flax lilies (*Dianella species)*, purple fountain grass, New Zealand flax (*Phormium species*) and Japanese blood grass.

- **SYNTHETIC TURFS** could be worth checking out if there's a small area of ground where you'd normally consider laying turf. The new generation of synthetic turfs actually look good, and when installed properly by a landscaper or qualified professional, require no extra care other than sweeping if the turf gets covered with leaves.

At the very least, you can probably expect to send in a gardener – or yourself – several times a year to trim any trees and do any additional maintenance required around the garden, so keep this in mind when reviewing your ongoing expense budget.

COURTYARD
A SIMPLE PAVED AREA ADDS VALUE TO YOUR RENTAL

HARDY PLANTS
REQUIRE MINIMUM
WATER

WILD GRASSES AND
SYNTHETIC TURF ARE
LOW MAINTENANCE

WHAT COULD GO WRONG?

If kids or dogs are likely to factor into your plans at some point, it's much easier to take them into account before you begin landscaping. Some features just don't mix with children and animals, no matter how good they look. Putting them in and then having to remove them – whether because of practicality or safety issues – is a very expensive path to go down, but with a bit of forethought, it can be easily avoided.

CHAPTER 3

...

YOUR FRONT GARDEN: FIRST IMPRESSIONS COUNT

The love it deserves

Your front garden is an important piece of real estate. It is the first thing anyone sees when they visit your house – and there is no doubt that a great front yard always makes a great first impression, and can make a home look and feel more appealing.

Unlike the backyard, which is usually more private, the front garden is often a space that doesn't see a lot of use. However, it *does* help create a real sense of home, given it's the last thing you see when you leave for work in the morning, and the first thing that greets you when you arrive home in the evening. So it is worth spending a bit of time, money and energy making your front garden inviting, calming and welcoming. Get it right and you'll start to relax whenever you see it.

From a real estate point of view, having a beautiful front garden, paired with a similarly attractive house facade, adds immeasurably to the value of your home. If you're planning on selling, you want to pull on the heartstrings of potential buyers and help them create an attachment to your house before they've even walked through the front door. This is most commonly referred to as 'kerb appeal' and is highly valued by real estate agents. We are very visual beings and often form opinions and emotions based on looks alone – so it isn't surprising that this also holds true when it comes to real estate.

RETHINKING THE FRONT YARD

It's not unusual for my clients to think of their front yard as a 'nothing area', but I always urge them not to overlook this vital space, and to ensure they've allocated an appropriate budget so we can make the most of what they have.

A cheap-looking front yard put together with little thought or care can create an instant impression for passers-by and visitors on the quality of the rest of your home – and usually it's not a good one. Although your builder might be happy to throw down wood chips dyed green as a makeshift front lawn or nature strip – minimal cost, and even less effort – it devalues the feel of the rest of your property, regardless of how well your house is built and how much money you've spent inside on fancy fittings and furnishings.

I mentioned earlier that it isn't necessary to pair the facade of your home with a garden design from a matching era, but this can definitely be of benefit when it comes to your front yard. Remember, too, that this is an area where a simple, neat design is often the most appealing, just as is often the case inside a home.

SIMPLE, CLEAN & SYMMETRICAL FRONT
GARDENS ARE A SOLID OPTION

KEEP COLOUR
REMOVABLE

Beware big personality clashes

Imagine walking into a house that has bold colours painted on the walls in every room, or bathroom tiles in a curdling shade of blood red. Potential buyers would walk through the front door and either turn around and leave immediately, or start adding up the costs of replacing all these unwanted features before pondering whether it's worth the extra cost and effort on top of the asking price. These sorts of decisions made by a homeowner can come into play when negotiations begin over the sale price. Compare this 'Should we, shouldn't we' and 'How much will it cost?' dilemma to a scenario where a potential buyer walks into a house with a neat, clean interior that is painted white. This makes it easy for them to visualise their own furniture, art and personal belongings filling the rooms. The latter is like a blank canvas, and there's often no competition when the choice is between a home like this and one that needs to have an owner's personality stripped from it.

The same concept also applies to the front garden. If an owner has filled the front garden in a haphazard fashion with trees and plants they love (regardless of whether they go together), to a potential buyer it might look like a complete mess. They'll be thinking about the money, time and effort involved in tidying up the garden by removing some trees and replacing them with others that are more appropriate.

When it comes to front gardens, simple, clean (and often symmetrical) designs have a similar effect to white walls inside a house – they won't polarise anyone who may want to buy your home in the future since the area can be enjoyed without the need to change anything.

PORTABLE SPLASHES OF COLOUR

One way to ensure you don't offend a future buyer's sensibilities is to keep colour removable. If you want to include flowers for impact, for example, try using them in pots or hanging baskets on either side of your front door. They'll offer some visual interest, but if they're not someone else's cup of tea when it comes time to sell, they can easily be removed.

ON THE FRONT FOOT

During the design and planning process, remember that it is worth spending enough time and money on your front garden so you can enjoy it every day. As well as adding long-term value to your home, it will always be there when you look out your window or walk through your front door. And it will always be there to greet you when you arrive home – rain, hail or shine.

How to create drive-by appeal

You shouldn't be completely driven by what your neighbours are up to, of course – but in a street full of weatherboard workers' cottages, you probably wouldn't build a huge two-level brick house with Grecian columns gracing a front portico. It works the same way with front gardens. Check out what some of the local residents have done, then decide which garden styles you like best and what would work with your level of commitment to maintenance. Remember, you do want to create 'wow' factor – but in the right way.

What do you do if no one in the street seems to give two hoots about how their front garden looks? Don't follow their lead and let your own front garden run to weeds. Go for smart and understated and you'll have the most desirable house in the street!

SYMMETRY IS PLEASING

Structure and symmetry seem to work best in front gardens. A well-structured garden is one in which all the elements appear well planned and executed with purpose, compared to one in which the various features appear to have randomly or haphazardly evolved, with a bit done here and another bit there. Symmetry is part of a structured design as it shows a balance

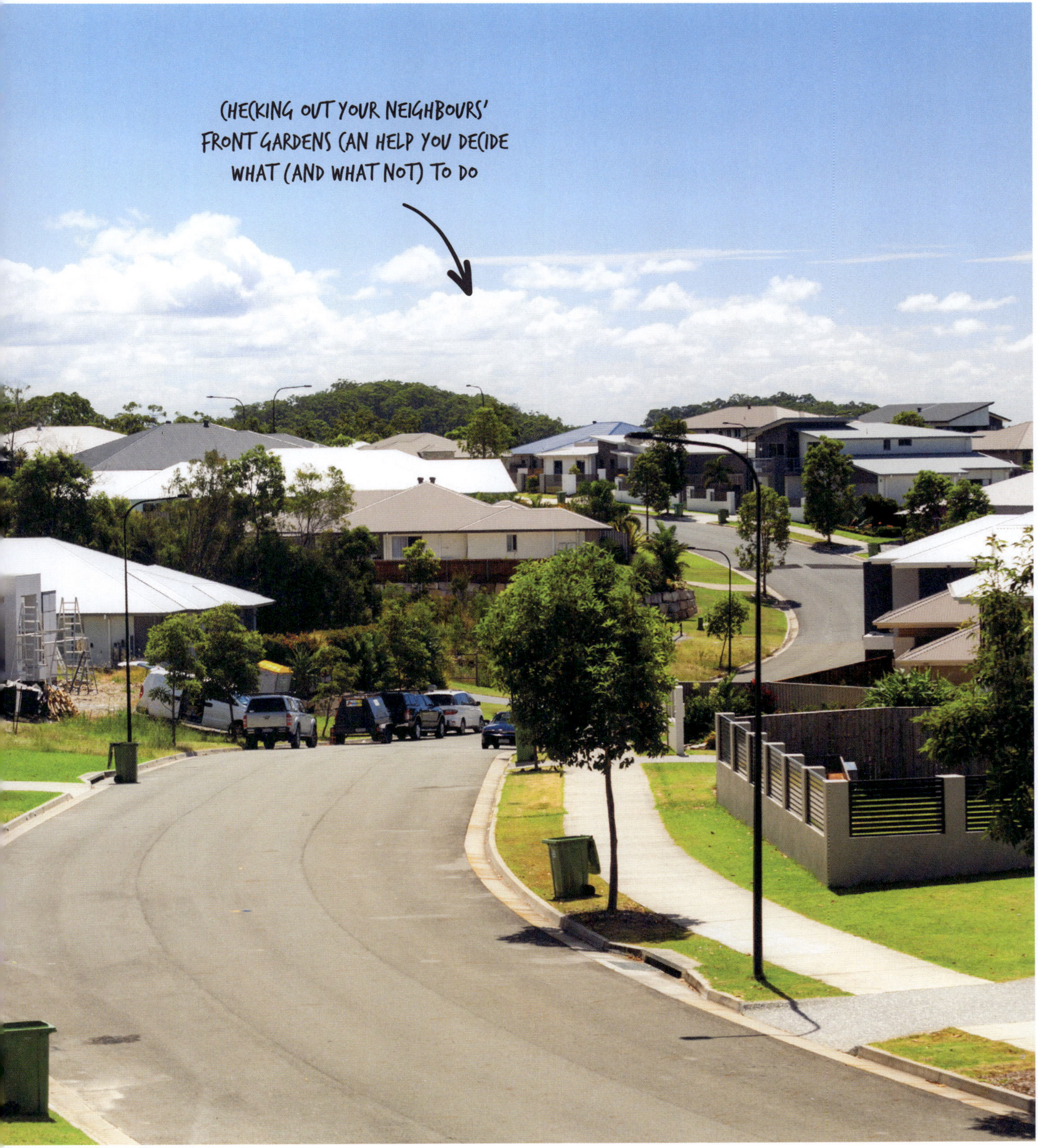
CHECKING OUT YOUR NEIGHBOURS' FRONT GARDENS CAN HELP YOU DECIDE WHAT (AND WHAT NOT) TO DO

THE FRONT DOOR IS
A CENTRAL FOCUS

PATHS ARE A VISUAL LEAD TO THE ENTRANCE

between paths, edging and plants, with a central focus on the front door.

Of course, when you look at the front of your house from the street, there's likely one thing that's going to throw the symmetry right off – the garage. But you can work around that, by treating the garage almost as if it's a different building. Use the facade of your home as the point to work from for your symmetrical garden design, and view the driveway and garage door as a separate zone to landscape. For example, if you have a row of ornamental pears planted along the fence line from your front fence to your garage, you don't have to match these along the opposite fence line of your front yard, as it's designed as a separate zone. Also, if you were to plant roses on either side of your front entrance path, you'd have that path central to your door, not central to the whole front of your property, which would include the garage.

UP THE GARDEN PATH ...

There are probably three main aspects to consider when it comes to the layout of your front garden. Top of your agenda should be the path leading from the street to your main entry door. On a practical level, this is a strong visual signal to visitors about where they should enter your house. You can heighten this effect by having big pots of coloured flowers on each side of your front door to further draw a visitor's eye.

... AND THROUGH THE FENCE AND GATE

Another good indicator of how to get into a home? The front gate. Which brings us to the second of your big garden considerations: the front fence. These days, not all houses even have a front fence, but if you have four-legged pets or small children, having a suitable fence around your property will help keep them safe, especially if you live on a busy street. In this case, it will also assist in keeping people and their pets off your garden or lawn.

What sort of fence you choose might depend on your budget, but some of the options include:

- Pickets
- Wire
- Metal
- Brick
- Stone
- High wooden fences.

Before you make a final decision and start building, it's worth checking with your local council to ensure there are no restrictions on fence heights and building materials in your area.

LOW PLANTS GO IN FRONT OF WINDOWS & HIGHER PLANTS IN BETWEEN

DAPHNE

CAMELLIA

DIETES

WESTRINGIA

LOMANDRA

GREVILLEA

GO WITH THE FLOW

The final piece of the puzzle is determining your plantings. Follow the structure of your house to determine where low plants and shrubs and taller trees can be used. Choose low plantings to go in front of windows, so they don't obstruct your view, while higher plantings can go in the spaces between windows. Mirror this along the fence line to add the symmetry the human eye finds so attractive.

EVERGREEN BEAUTIES

Lots of people plant roses or other flowers in their front garden, but these can be quite high maintenance. If you're not much of a gardener, you could instead try planting evergreens – they grow fast, don't need much water or much attention, and look almost as good during winter as they do during spring. Plus, choose the right ones and you'll have beautiful flowers at different times of year that will attract birds, bees and compliments. Great choices include daphne, camellias and dietes, as well as natives such as westringia, grevillea 'Amethyst' and lomandra 'Tanika'.

FLOWERS ARE NOT ONLY BEAUTIFUL, THEY ATTRACT BIRDS AND BEES

DIY SAVERS: A SPLASH OF COLOUR

It doesn't strictly fall into the category of landscape design, but a cheap and easy way to add a bit of interest to your front yard is to give your front door a fresh lick of paint in an attractive hue. Pale blues, greys and even bolder colours can really increase the street appeal of your home.

YOU WILL NEED

- Rubbing alcohol (optional)
- Screwdriver
- Fine sandpaper (around 180 grit)
- Clean sponge
- Painter's masking tape
- Drop sheet
- 1-litre tin of primer – oil-based if using an oil-based enamel paint, or a multipurpose water-based primer if using a water-based enamel paint. (A 4 litre tin offers far more value for money if other doors and elements also need painting at some point.)
- 2-litre tin of good-quality enamel exterior paint of your colour choice. A water-based one is easier to apply and clean up after, and is what we're using here. (Oil-based paints can be trickier to work with as all the brush strokes will be visible, so the paint will need to be applied using a straight 'up and down' action. You'll also need mineral turpentine for cleaning brushes afterwards.)
- A 50 mm high-quality angled sash cutter paint brush for decorative insets. (A quality one will cost a bit extra, but you won't be picking off brush hairs that have fallen into your paintwork.)
- Paint tray
- Small foam (or low nap) paint roller
- Cleaning rag for paint spills

HOW TO DO IT

1. If you're not sure what sort of paint was previously applied to the door, wipe over a bit of the existing paintwork with a little rubbing alcohol on a cotton ball. Does the paint come off? Then it's water based. If it doesn't come off, it's oil based.

2. Remove any decorative metal features, such as a mailbox slot or door knocker, using a screwdriver.

3. If the existing paintwork is in fairly good condition (just a few scratches; no flaking or mildew), you only need to give it a light sanding – which you can even do by hand, without a sanding block – so the new paint has good adhesion. If the original paint was oil based, you'll need to strip and/or sand it thoroughly. Be sure to clean up any residue off the floor.

4. Using a sponge and some water, clean the door, being sure to remove any remnants of the sanding. Let it dry.

5. Apply masking tape to the door's hinges, any inset glass, door knobs, locks, seals and surrounding door jambs to protect against accidental paint splashes.

6. Lay a drop sheet over the area beneath the door to catch any splashes.

7. Apply one coat of primer and let it dry.

8. Use a sash cutter first to paint any recesses on the first panel. Then use a small roller to cover the main area of the panel. Water-based paints dry fast, so cover these areas quickly, maintaining a wet edge so the finish is smooth.

9. Do one panel at a time, smoothing out any drips as you go so they don't set dry.

10. Once all the panels are finished, use the roller to paint the centre rail, followed by the centre stile. Overlap the painting strokes so they are smooth.

11. Next, paint the stiles on the outer edges of the door, the top rail and, finally, the bottom rail. Again, overlap the layers so they're smooth.

12. Rinse your brush and roller thoroughly under running water.

13. Allow the paint to dry completely before starting again at step 8 for a second coat; the door will need at least two coats all up.

14. When the door is completely dry, remove the masking tape and reattach the metal features.

DIY SAVERS: HIDING A METAL FENCE

When it comes to fences, metal ones are really affordable, but they often look quite hard and stark, and not very attractive. Luckily there is an easy way to hide an unsightly metal fence: by covering it with beautiful creepers and vines. They might take a little while to grow once you've planted them, but eventually you'll have that fence covered completely.

One of the most popular choices is jasmine, which smells heavenly when it blooms in spring; wisteria is another fragrant option that grows rampantly and is quite striking when it blooms. Potato vine, which bears beautiful white flowers in spring and summer, is another good choice.

In Australia, good endemic varieties include wonga-wonga vines and native sarsaparilla, which is available in a variety of colours.

WISTERIA

POTATO VINE

WONGA-WONGA

DIY SAVERS: A CONCRETE ALTERNATIVE

For garden pathways, concrete is often the material of choice. But if yours is cracked beyond repair, or you are laying down a new path from scratch, there is another option that is attractive, cheaper, and is something you can achieve yourself – crushed rock, overlaid with a layer of crushed granite.

Old concrete paths can be removed using a hired demolition saw, or a 9 inch angle grinder fitted with a diamond blade to cut the concrete into manageable sections for removal. Then use a sledgehammer to further break up the concrete into small liftable pieces.

Once the concrete has been removed, or you've dug out your new path, level it all out using a shovel, rake or lawn leveller. Then, all you need to do is top it with a 20 millimetre layer of crushed rock, level it out evenly, then top with a level 30 millimetre layer of crushed granite.

To work out how much crushed rock and crushed granite you'll need is simple. Measure out the length and width of your path in square metres, then multiply that by the depth required (in millimetres) to work out how many cubic metres you'll need. For example, say your path takes up 20 square metres:

- 20 square metres x 0.02 (20 mm depth) means you'll need 0.4 cubic metres of crushed rock.
- 20 square metres x 0.03 (30 mm depth) means you'll need 0.6 cubic metres of crushed granite.

However, bear in mind that you'll need a *minimum* 20 millimetre depth of crushed rock, after it's been compacted with a vibrating plate (you can hire these at hardware stores or machine hire plants, where you will also be given operating instructions). Then you need a minimum 30 millimetres of crushed granite on top, also compacted, so you'll need to order a little extra of each material to allow for the compression that occurs during compacting.

DEMOLITION SAW

ANGLE GRINDER

RAKING LEVEL

THE END RESULT –
ATTRACTIVE, AFFORDABLE
AND ACHIEVABLE

BUXUS HEDGES ARE A
CLASSIC CHOICE

MASS PLANTINGS OF LAVENDER
AND ROSES

Great garden beds

When designing your front yard, start by sketching out a map that you can draw on to plan your garden features.

Border beds planted along your front path can be really pretty and eye-catching. You can either use a low shrub that can be trained into a hedge shape (buxus is a good example), or a plant such as lavender if you love a few flowers and would like a beautiful smell to engulf your garden. Sticking to a single variety will give you a lovely abundant effect.

Garden beds don't have to be filled with flowers that require dead-heading and the spaces between them weeded. You can always plant taller trees interspersed with ground covers (good options are silver birch or olive trees with rosemary, creeping juniper or ivy), and spread the bare parts of the bed with organic mulch; if all goes well, the unplanted bits won't be bare for long. Organic mulch not only helps control weeds and reduce water evaporation, it also stops soil compacting over time – and unlike chunky wood chips, organic mulch slowly decomposes, ultimately enriching your garden's soil.

ORGANIC MULCH IS GREAT FOR ENRICHING YOUR SOIL AND CONTROLLING WEEDS

HANDY HERB POTS

STRAWBERRY

POTTED PLANTS ADD A PORTABLE SPLASH OF COLOUR AND CLASS

Containers and pots

If you have some sort of patio or low verandah along the front of your house, you can add planted interest using pots and planter boxes filled with potting mix. This is a perfect place to cultivate 'pops' of colour with flowers. It's much easier to keep them looking beautiful in confined spaces than out in the garden, and you won't have a problem with weeds.

You can also use your pots to grow herbs, spices and some fruits, which can be harvested for use in the kitchen. Great choices for pots include chives, basil, parsley, chillies and even strawberries.

Many pots and planter boxes don't come cheap, but they are an enjoyable easy-care gardening option. Just remember to water your plants regularly, and apply some liquid fertiliser now and then.

ADDING FLAIR TO PLAIN POTS

Large glazed pots, the sort you use as a feature element in a garden or courtyard, aren't always budget friendly. However, it is possible to buy plain terracotta or concrete pots and decorate them yourself. It doesn't have to be anything fancy or artistic, either. A couple of layers of carefully applied coloured paint can give a plain pot character.

A front-yard recreation zone

As housing blocks decrease in size, you may find you have more usable space in your front yard than at the back of the house. In this case, make the most of it by borrowing some of the backyard tips from the next few chapters and translating them to the front garden.

Planting a mature tree will give you an instant focal point. Plus, if it happens to be a productive variety, such as a citrus, it might even become a neighbourhood feature when the tree bears fruit and people come to separate you from your excess produce.

There's also no reason why you can't set a cafe table and chairs or a few beautiful Adirondack chairs on the verandah, or in a spot that catches the sun in the morning.

If you think you'll be using the front yard on a regular basis, remember to consider all your fencing options – particularly if you have children and pets, both in terms of keeping them safe and keeping the passing parade from encroaching on your turf.

A FRONT YARD LEMON TREE COULD BE A NEIGHBOURHOOD FAVOURITE

IF YOU USE YOUR FRONT YARD OFTEN, CONSIDER YOUR FENCING OPTIONS

WHAT COULD GO WRONG?

Most often, the biggest thing that can go wrong is spending your entire landscaping budget on your backyard, because you think that's where you'll spend the most time. But the front of your house is what the world sees – and it's also what *you* see every time you leave home and come back again. That doesn't mean your front yard needs equal billing with the one behind the house, but it should be an attractive space that feels welcoming. It will make you and your family happy – and further down the track, if you decide to move on, you'll have a lovely front yard that potential buyers will love, too. Create a good first impression early on and it will pay off for years to come.

CHAPTER 4

...

A SPACE FOR ALL SEASONS

When imagining their future garden, many people think of a lush space filled with flowers and birds. Which is what you might end up with – during spring. One of the biggest mistakes many people make is that they design for a single season, when many regions have four.

Australia, for example, is a country with quite extreme changes in temperature and conditions throughout seasons. Summer months can be extremely hot and dry, while winter can be very cold, with patches of wet weather that can often last for days. Spring is an ideal period to be outside enjoying outdoor spaces, while autumn brings short days with earlier nightfall and cooler nights. And that's just in the southern states. Head north and the climate changes completely. The tropical north is either hot and mostly dry – or hot and very wet.

This is one area in which a landscaper can be invaluable in the planning stages of your garden as they'll have a really good understanding about what plants suit your local climate and conditions.

Creating your all-season space

If you plan on getting use out of your outdoor area all year round, you'll need to cater for changing seasonal weather conditions in your landscape design.

COLD COMFORTS

In regions with cool autumns and chilly winters, having an undercover outdoor area or patio with some form of heating – whether that's a wood fire, gas fire or overhead electric heat strips – is pretty much essential if you're planning on using your outdoor space socially throughout colder days and nights.

Clients often suggest the idea of fire pits as a heating option, but these need to be in an open space that isn't undercover. In reality, as a social activity, they are much better suited to warmer nights than cold ones because they don't really offer a lot of heat. Fire pits often sit, unused and forlorn, in the middle of an outdoor area, taking up space that could better be used for a table or open area.

GETTING DECKED OUT

When planning a decking area, there are a number of options to consider. Many of the new build low-set homes come with a concrete slab with a patio roof over the top as part of the build package. This offers an entertaining area, but with a raw concrete finish it can seem cold and uninviting, especially given it is often set down a level from the internal house floor. An easy way to warm these areas up is to build a deck over them, which will also aid in making a seamless level between the inside of your home and outside, as you can match the two levels.

TAKING SHELTER

Having young children ourselves, my wife, Sophie, and I have really found the value in our undercover decking area. Our kids use it as their play space, so they don't feel confined to the indoors even on rainy days. The deck is surrounded by house walls on three sides. The fourth side is open, partitioned off with a timber balustrade. The open side faces south and hardly gets rain coming in. We see the deck as one of the best features of our home. Plus, there's nothing nicer than having an outdoor area where you take your cuppa and toast in the morning and read the news (or this book) with the birds singing around you.

Nearly all of these areas are set to the rear of the property, regardless of the home's orientation towards the sun and weather. This means some lucky residents will be afforded protection against the prevailing elements, while others will be facing the weather front on, which might require a pull-down screen or barrier to shield against wind and rain, or possibly sun shades at the height of summer.

Regardless of what you're working with, look at the different options to provide cover and shade.

If adding a roof to a new outdoor space will adversely reduce the amount of natural light entering living areas, you can look at options like pull-out patio shades, retractable patio roofs or polycarbonate roof panels such as LaserLite.

DECIDUOUS TREES PROVIDE A SHADE CANOPY IN SUMMER

FALLEN LEAVES ACT AS A NATURAL FERTILISER

JACARANDA

Choosing plantings: deciduous or evergreen?

Deciduous trees and shrubs add a natural all-season element to any garden. Their leaves turn a multitude of shades as the tree begins to go dormant during autumn, only to reveal bare trunks and branches throughout winter – which in themselves offer a striking sculptural appearance.

The loss of leaves also offers your garden other benefits, allowing more sunlight through to ground level, and giving lower-lying plants and lawns a much-needed energy boost through the winter frosts and short days, which can take their toll on many plants. It also allows this light and heat into nearby windows or onto exterior walls, giving your house an extra burst of warmth and light. Fallen leaves also act as a natural fertiliser as they decompose and release stored nutrients back into the ground, further aiding plant growth. Some popular deciduous trees include different varieties of maple and ash, as well as jacarandas, which have the added benefit of beautiful purple flowers during summer.

In the warmer months, when they are full of leaves, deciduous trees offer the opposite effect, providing a canopy to shade the same plants, lawns, windows and walls from the intense heat produced by the sun.

SUMMER SHADE,
AUTUMN SUN

Cover from the elements can also be achieved beneath an evergreen tree's canopy, which can be useful year round. The climate in which you live – and how your house and yard are orientated in relation to the sun – will determine whether deciduous or evergreen plants, or a mixture of both, are best suited to your garden. You'll also need to think about how much time you want to spend maintaining the garden. Evergreen trees will still drop leaves over the course of the year, but not en masse as deciduous ones do in autumn, so you won't notice them as much, and they'll require far less raking.

Making maximum use of the changing seasons

When designing an outdoor space, think of how you'll be using it from one season to the next.

Clever multi-purpose spaces with versatile surfaces can accommodate many changes of use between seasons.

For example, in warmer months, a level area surfaced with vehicle pavers with grass growing between them can be used as a larger play or outdoor dining area. During winter, when the grass dies back and the area isn't used as frequently, the same space can be used to store items such as trailers or boats. These can then be moved out again as the weather warms up and the items are put to more regular use again.

Seating structures that can be moved undercover when the weather isn't great, or out onto the lawn when it is sunny and warm, work well. So does box seating that can open up and provide storage for outdoor cushions, toys or sporting equipment – these are great options for families who have a lot of stuff that needs somewhere to live.

VEHICLE PAVERS & GRASS
PROVIDE A FUNCTIONAL SPACE
FOR ALL SEASONS

BOX SEATING THAT CAN OPEN
UP PROVIDES EXTRA STORAGE

A POOL PROVIDES MANY HOURS
OF SUMMER FUN

SOLAR HEATING CAN EXTEND
THE DIPPING SEASON

To pool, or not to pool?

If you have a family and live in a hot climate, there can be a lot of pressure to install a pool when you're landscaping the backyard. But don't cave in to the pressure until you've fully investigated what it's going to cost – both in the actual construction of the pool, and in the considerable time and expense involved maintaining it.

ADDING UP THE NUMBERS

It probably shouldn't come as a surprise that pools are expensive, especially the in-ground concrete numbers to which most people aspire. But don't take the quoted cost at face value. Have you got easy access for the excavator and concrete truck? Does the price include excavation, as well as all the pumps, vacuums and other accoutrements you'll need to run the pool? Do you need to build a little shed to protect the pump and store all the chemicals you'll need to keep it clean? Have you factored in the cost of the mandatory fence required to enclose it?

If you've done all that, looked at your budget and worked out that you can still afford it, you should then consider all the other factors involved in owning a pool.

COUNTING THE DAYS

The value of a pool is tied to how often you are going to use it. If you live in a warm climate, there are probably more days in the year when you'll jump in the pool and love it than days where it will remain unused. Travel to more temperate zones, though, and it might be that you're skimming leaves and treating it like a giant water feature for six months at a time – or covering it entirely so that you don't have to deal with it. If you've got extra cash in your budget, you can look at solar heating systems to make the water a bit warmer for longer into winter each year.

ADDING UP THE HOURS

It's true that pools are an amazing way to entertain kids. They'll spend all day in there with friends during summer school holidays and on warm afternoons. No matter what they tell you, though, they won't help you look after it. Maybe for the first few weeks, but you can be sure it'll be the adults doing all the hard yards – keeping an eye on pool safety, cleaning it, monitoring water quality, adding chemicals, running to the pool shop for supplies – so make sure you've got the time to give a pool the love it needs.

A FINAL WORD OF ADVICE

Remember that if you plan on selling your home further down the track, potential buyers may not be as keen on the pool as you and your family were. They could instead view it as an effort they don't want to have to deal with, and either cross your property off their list immediately or try to bargain the asking price down so they have enough money left to cover the cost of having the pool filled in. After all, pools take up a lot of room in a backyard – space that could be used for more lawn, paved areas or garden beds.

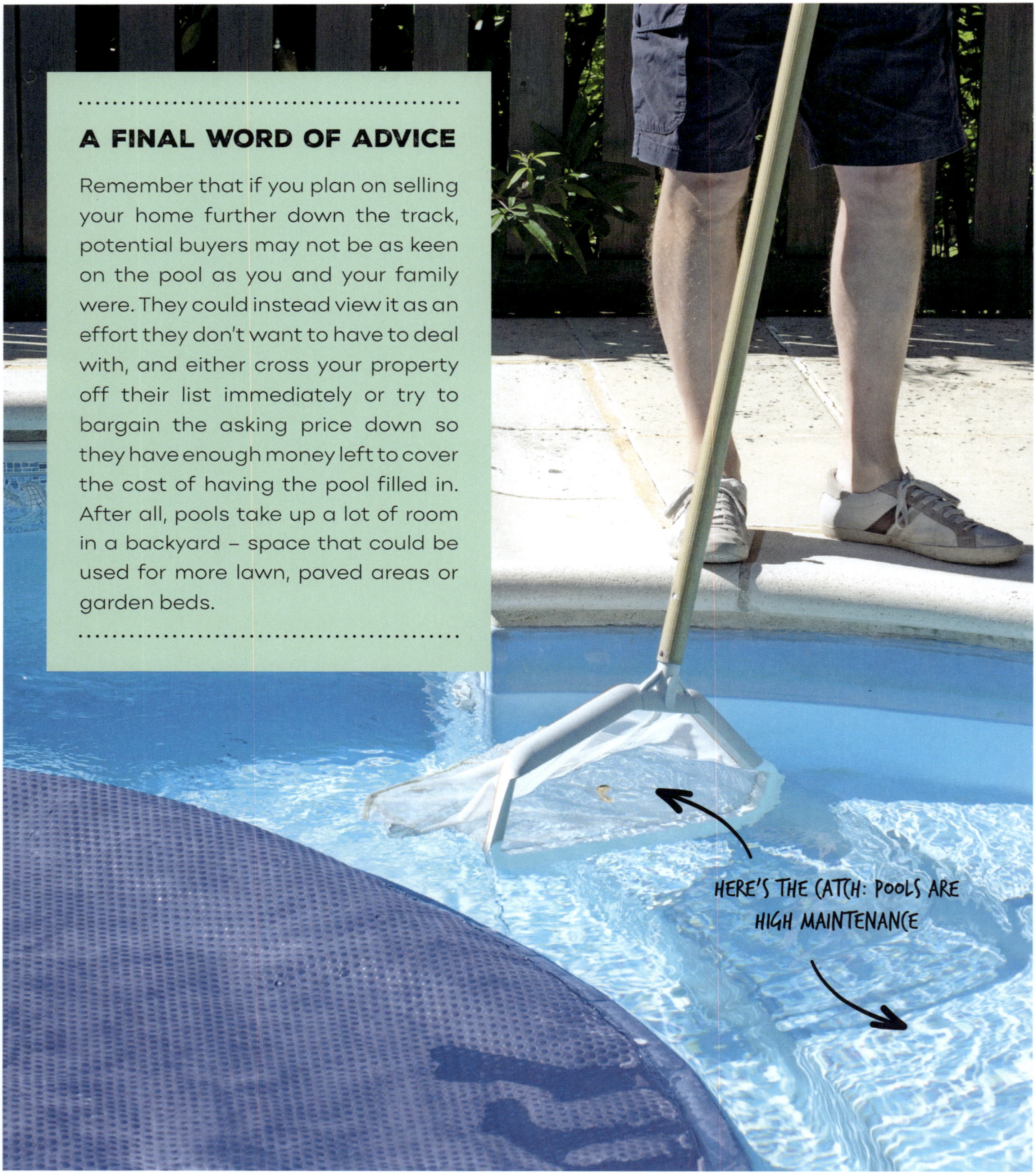

WHAT ABOUT A SWIM SPA?

If you're not sure about having a pool but are a keen lap swimmer, another option to investigate might be a swim spa. These can be heated year round, are often a more effective way to keep fit than an average backyard pool (you swim continuously against strong jets of water), and can be relocated if you decide to move house or no longer want it. They don't come cheap, however: in Australia, a swim spa big enough for one person to swim in, or three adults to relax in, will cost about $22,000. On top of this, you'll have installation and maintenance costs (including treating the water and cleaning the filters), plus any heating costs (some people have solar, which is less expensive than running the heater off the mains power). Most swim spas are installed outdoors, but installing one inside is also an option if you have an indoor space large enough.

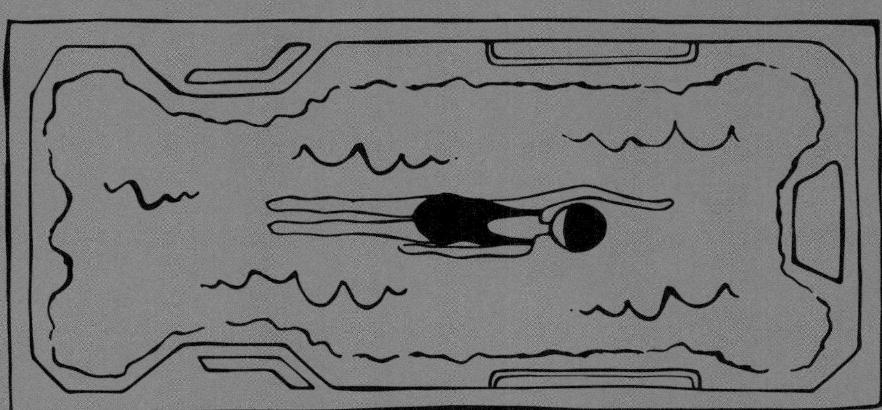

WHAT COULD GO WRONG?

Not accounting for all the seasons will likely lead to creating a garden that can only be used at certain times of the year. That's a lot of wasted space you could be enjoying year-round. Get the plantings wrong and you could end up with an evergreen canopy that blocks essential light and warmth to the rest of the garden and your house during the winter months. On the other hand, not having any shade-bearing trees or an undercover area will mean the garden becomes too hot to use during the height of summer, when most people want to be outdoors. The last thing you want to do is spend a lot of money on a backyard that simply doesn't work for you, and that you can't get the maximum enjoyment and benefit from.

CHAPTER 5

...

THE OUTDOOR ROOM

It's become a buzzword that real estate agents and interior designers are rather fond of, but the idea of an 'outdoor room' is one that makes sense. Why have lots of outdoor space if you're not going to use it as regularly as your living room?

The whole idea, though, of an 'outdoor room' is to make it completely comfortable, and somewhere you feel drawn to from the moment you wake up in the morning until retiring to bed at night.

An outdoor room is not just about entertaining, although for many this is highly desirable. Ideally, the yard is a place where you can relax, play, entertain, and even cook or work (if you put in an outdoor kitchen with a barbecue, and create a space to bring your laptop to enjoy the sunshine if you work from home some of the time). The outdoor room should also enjoy generous views of the rest of your garden, and preferably blend in harmoniously with it. After all, its purpose is to link your lifestyle to your garden throughout the year and draw you to nature for relaxation.

Making it private

For most people, privacy is high on their list of needs when designing a garden. New estates and inner-city homes tend

CREATE PRIVACY USING CLEVER PLANTINGS

to have a lot of overlooking windows from neighbouring properties, and a lack of established trees, which can make people reluctant to spend time enjoying their outdoor spaces. After all, who wants the neighbours to be able to see everything they're doing, every minute of the day?

A CUSHIONING SCREEN

Rather than spending money on built structures, creating privacy using clever plantings is a simple yet effective option. An established tree canopy can furnish an outdoor area with beautiful shade and privacy, while also providing the 'softening' effect that only foliage can deliver. A roofed structure constructed for privacy, on the other hand, can appear quite hard and unnatural, and is less relaxing to the eye, besides being the more expensive option.

FAST-GROWING SPECIES FOR SHADE OR PRIVACY

When you're starting a garden from scratch, choosing trees and plants that grow quickly will help make your outdoor spaces feel more established in what seems like no time at all. Of course, not all plants work in all climates and soil types, but here are five varieties you might want to consider if you need shade or privacy fast. If these ones are not available, check with your local nursery or garden expert to see what other options would suit your needs. Species of cypress, laurels and photinia might fit the bill, and holly trees, thuja (*Arborvitae*) and evergreen magnolia cultivars are also an option.

LILLY PILLY

JAPANESE MAPLE

PITTOSPORUM TENUIFOLIUM

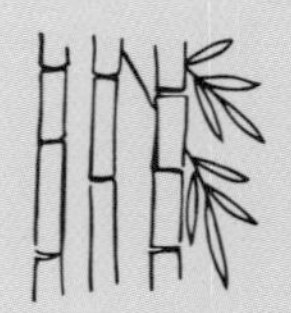

CLUMPING BAMBOO

CALLISTEMON

LILLY PILLY There are lots of different types of this native Australian tree – but all of them are hardy and grow in either sun or shade as long as they have moist, well-drained soil. The Bush Christmas lilly pilly grows to about 6 metres (unless it's pruned regularly) and is great for creating a wind break, hedge or screen. The new foliage starts out orange before turning green, and produces white flowers in spring, and red fruit in summer.

JAPANESE MAPLE These are great in a cooler climate, and like rich, well-drained soil and protection from harsh suns and strong winds. Again, there are many different varieties, with many growing to 4–5 metres. The delicate leaves change colour in autumn, before dropping to the ground.

PITTOSPORUM TENUIFOLIUM Known in its native New Zealand as kohuhu or black matipo, this tree is even hardier than a lilly pilly. Small, dense leaves and the ability to quickly grow to 3–5 metres means they make great screening plants.

CLUMPING BAMBOO Got a small area that requires fast screening? This is a good hardy choice that can also look sculptural and interesting. It can take a couple of years to get started, but once it does, it will grow up to 4 metres tall. Other 'running' species of bamboo might actually grow faster – but they can get out of control quite quickly, too, and even invade gardens several houses down the street!

CALLISTEMON More popularly known as bottlebrushes, these robust Australian native varieties grow fast and thick to a height of up to 10 metres. They offer excellent screening from neighbours or the street, and their flowers – mainly red but also sometimes pink or mauve – attract nectar-feeding native birds such as wattlebirds and honeyeaters.

WEEPING LILLY PILLY

PHOTINIA

A TALL HEDGE PROVIDES AN EFFECTIVE
BACKDROP FOR A SMALLER HEDGE

PITTOSPORUM

CASUARINA

HEDGE FUNS

Hedges along your fence line can also create a great privacy screen from overlooking neighbours, and even block out an unsightly view of the neighbouring property itself. They also work well as a backdrop to smaller plantings in front of them. The hedge itself could literally be any thickly planted row of tall shrubs, providing a solid backdrop (much like a dark painted fence) that allows any smaller plants in front to stand out – even if the smaller plants are just another shade of green. A plant with striking flowers would pop out even more with a green hedge behind it.

There are many varieties of trees and plants that can be grown to form a privacy barrier along the boundary of your property. Some form very dense thick hedges that need more trimming and maintenance – such as conifer species, weeping lilly pilly (*Waterhousea floribunda*), photinia 'robusta' and pittosporum 'James Stirling'. Others – such as clumping bamboo (non-running varieties) and casuarina, banksia and grevillea species – are a little more whimsical and less structured, but will probably need little maintenance, particularly once they're established.

DIY SAVERS: HOW TO PLANT A HEDGE FOR SCREENING AND PRIVACY

Straight lines, a single type of plant ... It's a simple plan, and one that most people who can work a shovel can do. Here's how.

YOU WILL NEED

- Plants – how many you need will depend on the desired length of your hedge and the growth habit of the plant you have chosen, so check with your local nursery or garden expert if you're unsure
- Shovel
- Compost if you have it (a good handful per plant), or a slow-release fertiliser
- Seaweed solution or liquid fertiliser. 2–3 litres will make up more than enough for a decent-sized hedge
- Watering can
- Hedge clippers or electric shears

HOW TO DO IT

1. First, mark out where each plant will go. I usually sit the plants in place in their pots until I'm happy with their spacing.

2. Next, dig the holes for planting. Each hole will need to be slightly larger than the pot the plant came in. Remember, planting the plants closer together will make them grow into each other more quickly, so they'll form a dense hedge or privacy screen more rapidly and will then start growing taller to your desired height. Otherwise, when planted further apart, you may have to keep trimming the tops to encourage the plants to grow wider for the hedge to form.

3. Put a handful of compost (or slow-release fertiliser) into each of the holes.

4. Carefully tip a plant out of its pot, then carefully tease out the roots with your fingers to free them up a little. Place the plant into its hole, then move the soil that's already been dug out back into the hole to fill it. Press the soil down gently. Repeat with all the plants.

5. Dilute some seaweed solution in a watering can (the label will outline how much to add to each litre of water), then apply some to each of the plants.

6. Give your plants a few months to grow, then start trimming them, in a straight line across the top, to form the shape of the hedge. As a general guide, trim the hedge about three to five times a year – or more often if you're trying to maintain a smaller height and width, such as alongside a driveway.

PERGOLA OF DELIGHTS

Don't write off the idea of incorporating a pergola or other roofed alfresco area right from the start. Along with privacy, they offer a pleasant sheltered outdoor seating area from which to enjoy your garden, even during rain. If you live in a region that experiences downpours on a regular basis, one of these will be most invaluable. Is there anything better than sitting outside during a storm, watching the rain come down and the lightning flashing, and smelling all that ozone being created, while you're undercover, dry and warm? No matter how thick a canopy of big trees becomes, it will never completely shield you from the rain and wind in the same way a pergola does.

If you want to get the most out of your yard, you definitely need to have places where you can sit out of the harsh sun and rain, and away from the prying eyes of neighbours.

The garden essentials

One of the challenges when incorporating an outdoor room into a backyard design is that you still need to include all the practicalities expected in a backyard, some of which aren't necessarily the most beautiful things you'll ever see.

CLOTHES LINES

Anyone who has a family will know the importance of having a clothes line, and how much better it is to dry clothes in the sun and wind whenever possible, rather than in an electric dryer. It's better for the environment as well as the clothes – they smell fresher and last longer when dried naturally.

The traditional Hills Hoist freestanding rotary clothes line is an Australian icon, but they do take up a lot of space, so they're not exactly practical if you only have a small area to work with. (You'll have kids and dogs running through the clean washing, so you'll end up having to wash it all again!)

However, there are several types of clothes lines that you can easily pull out of sight when you're not using them, to give yourself more room and make the backyard look a lot neater.

Retractable clothes lines are fixed to a wall or fence and are simply pulled out and hooked on to another wall or post when you want to use them. They are available with six lines that extend about 6.5 metres, which is easily enough room to hang out sheets and towels – and these models are relatively inexpensive.

There are also fold-down clothes lines that attach to the wall of the house or an area of the back fence – preferably not on a wall that never sees the sun if you're in a colder region, or nothing will ever dry in winter. You can get these models in a variety of sizes up to about 3.3 metres wide and extending to a maximum of about 2 metres. They don't have quite as much room for hanging as a rotary clothes line, but are an excellent option for townhouses and villas with small outdoor areas as you can click them down flat when they're not needed. They're easy to use, too, and require only one person to operate. The biggest versions offer about 39 metres of total hanging space.

BARBECUES

For many of us, it wouldn't be a proper backyard without somewhere to cook a sausage or steak, so another prized outdoor feature is often a barbecue. Some people build one in, but that can be expensive;

FOLD-DOWN CLOTHES LINES
ARE A GREAT OPTION FOR
SMALL OUTDOOR AREAS

most simply have a gas barbecue, whether it's a tiny two-burner model or one of those giant contraptions with a wok ring and a hood. Only you know how often you'll cook on it, and how big it will need to be.

When you're using it, you want it to be out of the wind and rain. It should be far enough away from windows so that it doesn't splash grease everywhere, yet close enough to the kitchen so that when you realise you forgot the paper towel it's not a five-minute return journey to fetch it. The beauty of a portable barbecue is that you can move it around as needed.

It should also go without saying that barbecues work best on a hard, flat surface. They can damage lawns, so you want to make sure there's a dedicated paved or decked area where you can set it up for cooking.

GOING THE WHOLE HOG: THE OUTDOOR KITCHEN

Installing a full outdoor kitchen set-up is becoming increasingly popular. Alongside a barbecue, you can build in all the fittings you'd find in your indoor kitchen – including other cooktops, cupboards and drawers, sinks and fridges. If you're the sort of family who uses the gas barbecue five nights a week and practically lives outdoors, you might get a lot of use (and therefore value) from a fit-out such as this. It's also great if your family really loves entertaining – it means you can host parties almost completely outdoors and not have vast groups of people traipsing around inside the house.

These beauties come at a cost, though. A full set-up, with all the bells and whistles, can cost tens of thousands of dollars. Alternatively, you can go to a specialist barbecue or hardware store and buy a prefabricated outdoor kitchen – some of which include cooktops, cupboards, benchtops and a sink – for several thousand dollars. You'll need to have it properly installed though, so that it hooks up to the gas mains and the water mains.

GARDEN SHEDS

The final must-have in many backyards is secure weatherproof storage or a garden shed. If you're lucky enough to have a really big garage, you might be able to set it up so that you can store your mower and other garden equipment in there.

If you need some extra room to keep garden equipment, kids' toys and other bits and pieces out of the weather, it's worth considering a small garden shed. Head down to your local hardware store and you'll discover they come in a range of sizes, from not much bigger than a large cupboard to somewhere large enough to park a boat. Many are made from metal sheeting such as Zincalume, but more expensive varieties are available in timbers such as cedar. Some have windows, but for others you'll need a torch when you're rummaging around inside.

When you're budgeting for a shed, don't forget to add in the cost of putting down a concrete slab (if it's a small shed, you could put it over a paved area), adding some internal shelves, and connecting electricity. What you don't want to do is erect the shed on a bit of lawn and just throw everything inside. For a start, you'll never be able to find anything, plus it might end up attracting insects and other pests.

Other little extras

PLAY AREAS

If you have kids, and a decent area to work with, these 'little extras' might not be little at all, and you can look at additions like trampolines, swing sets, slides, cubby houses and sandpits. Anything that encourages kids to spend time playing outside, away from their electronic devices and screens, is always worth the investment. Remember that kids outgrow these different kinds of play equipment, so it's worth checking the local and online classifieds for good-quality second-hand outdoor play sets.

Besides being a suitable size for your garden, the most important aspect when choosing play sets is safety.

If you're installing a swing set or trampoline yourself, the first step is to ensure they are anchored correctly. There should be a large open area around the swing set or trampoline. It shouldn't be near any fences or the house – just in case someone gets flung off or decides to use the swing or trampoline to climb to the top of the fence and jump (or fall!) off. There also needs to be a large area of soft surface beneath, at least 30 centimetres thick, and extending for another 2.5 metres beyond the limits of the swing or trampoline's arc.

Basically, if you have kids, you want your outdoor space to have as much appeal as the room indoors where the TV lives. If they've got places to play, hide, catch bugs or fill up an inflatable pool, they might be happy to spend as much time outside in the sunshine and fresh air as they do watching Netflix or playing *Fortnite*.

FIRE PITS

I've mentioned fire pits in a previous chapter, but they are worth discussing again. Lots of clients ask me about them, thinking they'll be a cosy option on cold nights. In reality, fire pits are more about gathering around than heating. People are drawn to fire after dark, and fire pits make a great spot to sit around and talk when you've invited friends and family to your house.

Fire pits that are properly built in – and they can even be connected to a gas source, so you don't have to worry about collecting firewood – do take up quite a bit of space that can't be used for anything else. Not surprisingly, depending on whether you build them from stone or brick, they can also be quite expensive.

If a fire pit appeals, it's worth checking out some of the more affordable portable versions. That way, when you're not using it, you can stash it in the garage or shed and use the space for something else. Portable

PLACE SWINGS AND TRAMPOLINES
IN A LARGE OPEN AREA
AWAY FROM THE HOUSE AND
ANY FENCES

A PORTABLE FIRE PIT MAY BE A MORE USEFUL, COST-EFFECTIVE OPTION

fire pits generally come in two styles: a deeper brazier that wood can be stacked into, and shallow ones with a metal grill cover to stop coals and sparks being blown onto the ground.

Regardless of what type you choose, you'll want a paved area to put it on, as hot coals and bits of glowing wood will drop through or fall out, damaging any lawn underneath. Having a stone or concrete surface beneath a portable fire pit also makes it much easier to sweep up any soot and charcoal the next day.

Always make sure a fire pit is fully extinguished before you head off to bed for the night.

DIY SAVER:
HOW TO BUILD A SANDPIT

Little kids love sandpits, and luckily they are very easy to install in your backyard. Apart from the space, all you really need is a set of timber sleepers and the sand to fill the pit. The following instructions are for a square sandpit measuring 2 metres along each side, giving a play area of 4 square metres.

When buying the timber sleepers, avoid treated pine – you don't want arsenic nasties near your kids.

YOU WILL NEED

- Four x 2.4 metre timber sleepers (not treated pine), cut to your desired length (2 metres), either at the hardware store, or using a circular saw – remembering to cut the thickness of the sleepers (e.g. 50 millimetres or 75 millimetres) off two of the sleepers, to keep the finished size 2 metres x 2 metres
- Measuring tape
- Spray can of chalk dye
- Shovel
- Spirit level (optional)
- A 25-litre bag of scoria, if drainage is an issue
- Eight x 125 mm galvanised batten screws (you'll be using two screws in the end of each sleeper to attach them all together, so you'll need 8 screws in total)
- Cordless impact driver
- Electric or battery-operated sanding plane
- Coarse sand. You'll want to fill your sandpit with about 15 centimetres of sand and leave about 5 centimetres of the sleeper above sand level to keep the sand contained and stop it spilling out. This means that for a sandpit covering 4 square metres, you'll need about 0.6 cubic metres of sand ($4\ m^2 \times 0.15 = 0.6\ m^3$)

HOW TO DO IT

1. Find a good, flat part of the backyard – preferably somewhere out of the way, but an area you can still see from the kitchen or back window so you can keep an eye on the kids when they're playing in the sandpit. You don't necessarily want to place the sandpit under a tree either, particularly a fruit tree. It's one thing to have a bit of shade and to occasionally have to rake leaves from the sandpit, it's quite another to have to relieve it of rotting, fallen fruit.

2. Mark out the boundary of the sandpit using chalk dye, then start digging it out to remove the lawn and its roots, down to a depth of 20 centimetres. You can use any turf you cut out to repair bare patches in your lawn, or put it into your compost bin, grass-side down. Scatter any topsoil you dig out over any garden beds. Make sure the bottom of the pit is flat; visually by eye is fine, but you could also use a spirit level.

3. If you dig and discover the soil below is hard clay, you'll need to sort out some drainage. The easiest way is to dig a 20 centimetre–deep hole in the middle of the pit, fill it almost to the top with scoria, then top it off to level with a little bit of dirt. During heavy downpours, this will allow any rainwater that collects in the pit to naturally drain away into the soil, keeping the sand as dry as possible.

4. Get someone to help you lay the timber sleepers out – they'll be heavy – then use galvanised batten screws and a cordless impact driver to screw the sleepers into shape. It's best to do this in place, since the whole structure will be heavy and awkward to move into position once it's screwed together. For safety, I always then plane the sharp top edges off all the sleepers to round them off, making them friendlier for children's play spaces.

5. The final step is to fill the pit with sand. If your backyard has good access, you can order it in bulk and have a truck deliver it, otherwise you can buy 20-litre bags of coarse sand at soil centres. (It is much cheaper to fill bags provided by your sand and soil centre yourself, rather than to pay for pre-filled bags.)

It's a good idea to also knock up a sandpit cover – not so much for rain protection, but to stop the pit from becoming the local kitty litter box. A tarpaulin that can be secured with eyelets works perfectly well.

Growing your own

VEGIE PATCH

If you have a bit of space – and you don't even need a lot – you can join a growing trend and devote parts of your garden to producing some of your own vegetables and herbs. Many people are opting for raised garden beds, which can be constructed from a frame of timber sleepers or coated metal sheeting. All you need to do is assemble the planter frames, put them in their desired spot, fill them with soil suitable for propagating plants, and add some seedlings. These raised planters come in a huge variety of sizes, including long narrow ones if you're working within the confines of a small courtyard.

Small, elevated garden beds made from galvanised steel are also available, which are great for kids to look after, as well as anyone who has issues with their back or knees; some of these look like galvanised water tanks cut in half. I've even installed vertical garden panels, dedicated to herbs and suitably compact fruits, such as strawberries. There are heaps of different types of these, made from all kinds of materials; any one of them would work fine. If using wood, just ensure it is untreated.

ELEVATED STEEL BEDS

VERTICAL HERB GARDEN

RAISED GARDEN BEDS

ROCKET

LETTUCE

CARROTS

RADISHES

SNOW PEAS

GREEN BEANS

The great thing about vegies is that many varieties are really easy to grow. Tomatoes, rocket, lettuce, carrots, radishes, snow peas and green beans are all well within the capabilities of a gardening newbie, as are strawberries.

If you've got a little bit of time to invest in a vegetable garden, the rewards are many. Apart from saving money when your crops ripen, you'll discover they also taste a lot fresher than the produce you buy at the supermarket.

MAGIC WORMS AND BRILLIANT COMPOST

When you're plotting out space for a vegetable patch, you might also want to consider installing a compost bin and/or a worm farm. Both of these will reduce your household waste, reduce your greenhouse emissions (rotting organic waste in landfill produces environmentally harmful gases) and provide you with excellent nutrients for the soil in your garden.

Some local councils even offer a discount or free delivery on compost bins and worm farms when you buy them from websites like Compost Revolution, so check what's on offer in your area.

CHICKENS

Keeping chickens has become another popular backyard activity. Not only do chickens produce eggs, they also love all your kitchen leftovers, such as meat scraps and vegetable peels, so you won't have to worry about disposing of them ever again. Plus, chickens get used to their humans quite quickly and will cheerily peck and cluck around the backyard and come when you call them with food. Many people get quite devoted to their chickens and find being able to watch and hear them relaxing.

If you have good, high fences and no other pets that will give them grief, chickens will quite happily scratch around in the backyard. If you don't want to give them the run of the lawn, you can always create or buy a moveable coop – called a 'chicken tractor' – that lets them scratch and peck securely in a certain area for a while before you move the coop to a fresh patch of grass to allow the remaining yard to recover.

Chickens do always need to be locked up somewhere they can roost at night. Plenty of companies make prefabricated coops with nest boxes and roosts; some even have automated timers that open the chicken coop door in the morning, so you don't have to remember to let the girls out each day! All you need to do is supply fresh, clean straw on the floor and in the nests, along with food and fresh water every day.

Local councils have strict regulations about how many and what sort of chickens you can keep in a backyard, so check the specific rules relating to your neighbourhood. Many councils will also require coops to be set a certain distance from houses and boundary fences, and you'll have to agree to keep the coop and yard clean and store food properly so as not to attract pests.

Needless to say, no suburban councils will allow roosters to be kept in residential areas. Regardless of how well you get on with the neighbours, nothing will set up a local feud like people being woken each morning by pre-dawn crowing!

WHAT COULD GO WRONG?

Gardens, much like other rooms in the house, can be jaw-droppingly beautiful – but if you and your whole family don't enjoy them, what really is the point? Integrating fun and useful elements into the garden will make you want to spend loads of time out there, especially if you design it to be useable throughout the year. Just make sure that you plan ahead and have all the permissions you need from your local council to ensure your outdoor room is safe and isn't going to encroach on your neighbours' enjoyment of their own backyard.

MAKE SURE YOU HAVE THE NECESSARY PERMISSIONS BEFORE STARTING YOUR DREAM OUTDOOR SPACE

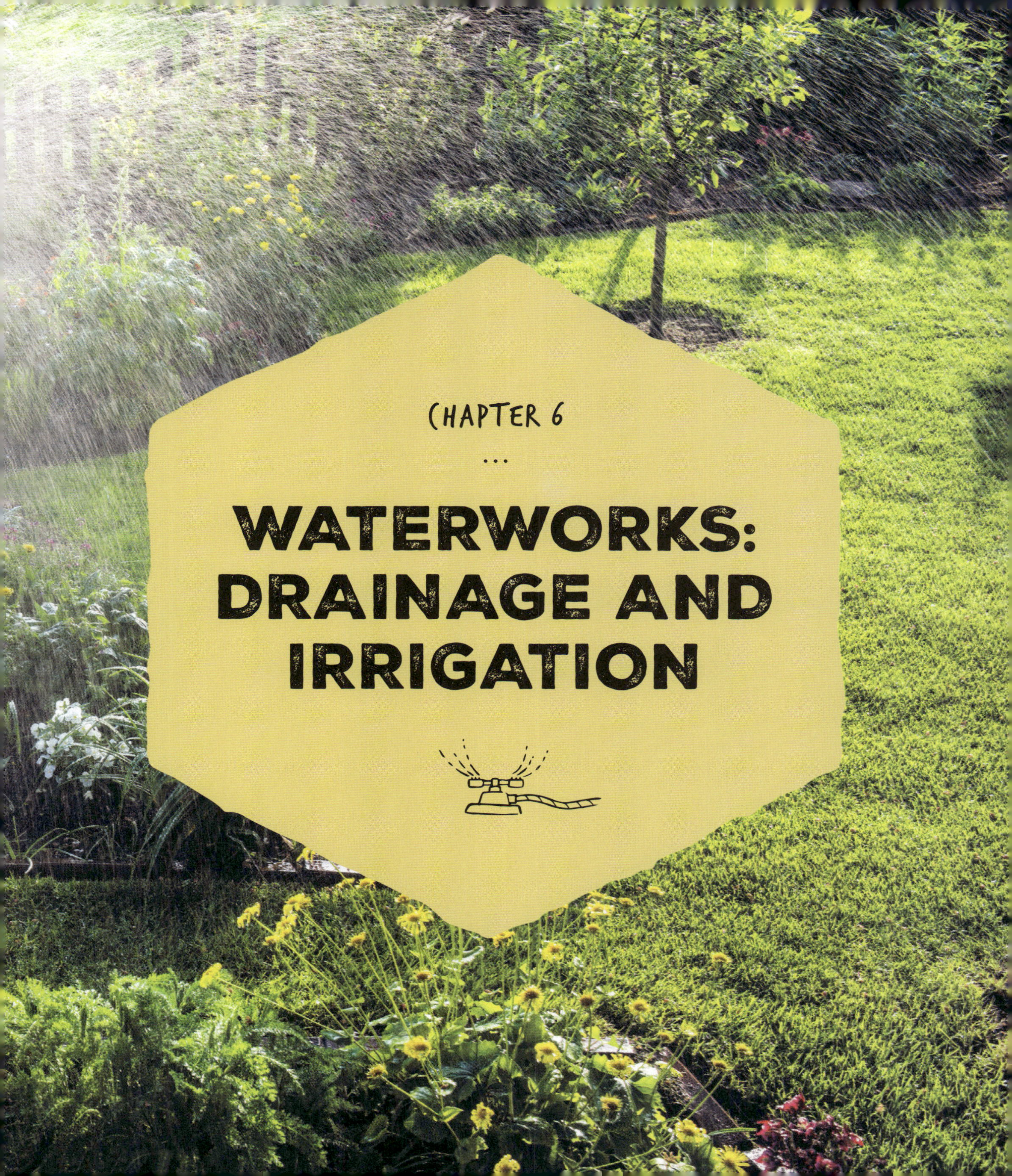

CHAPTER 6

WATERWORKS: DRAINAGE AND IRRIGATION

Believe me, I can see it from here. Reading the title of this chapter, your eyes just began to glaze over. But if you want to have a beautiful garden everyone loves spending time in, you also need to take into account some underlying fundamental practicalities you can't really see – such as how water gets to the garden, and how it drains away.

Take care of essentials such as drainage and irrigation in your initial garden designs – it'll pay off big time, saving you a lot of time, expense and trouble in the long run.

Delving into drainage

Soil is a permeable surface. Rain and water absorb into it, then eventually drain away into the underlying water table. This completely natural process happens at different rates, depending on what sort of soil lies beneath your turf.

WHERE DOES ALL THE WATER GO?

Drainage is a vital aspect in all outdoor spaces, especially those surrounding and adjoining your dwelling's walls. If you build up or excavate areas around your home, it is incredibly important to consider where water will sit, pool or naturally drain to if there are heavy downpours. A good-

WATER NEEDS SOMEWHERE TO GO

looking landscape is useless if it doesn't have appropriate drainage to ensure your home's foundations aren't damaged by excess water.

DIVERTING THE FLOW

You also need to take into account drainage on hard surfaces you add to a garden, such as paving and driveways. These areas hold water on the surface, much in the same way as the roof on a house collects water. The run-off needs to be diverted to stormwater, or preferably dispersed or drained towards an underground tank for storage and future use.

FALLING AWAY

Landscapers will create what we call 'fall', which ensures surface water flows towards a drain. Whether you're talking about permeable surfaces (such as soil and turf) or impermeable surfaces (such as concrete), when it comes to landscaping surrounding or adjoining a house, the fall *always* has to be *away* from the dwelling.

There are occasional exceptions, such as when a steep driveway runs down towards a garage, in which case a full grate drain should be installed to catch all the run-off before it gets to your garage.

WHAT LIES BENEATH

Decks are another common landscaping element that can be semi-permeable – they collect water on the surface, but excess water can also run off through the gaps between boards to be absorbed naturally underneath the deck's frame.

With these sorts of structures, much like retaining walls, it is important to have sub-surface drainage (such as agricultural pipes) to remove excess water sitting in the soil surrounding decking posts. This allows the excess water to drain into stormwater faster, so the posts holding up your deck (or retaining wall) don't become water damaged, which will shorten their lifespan.

WATER-DAMAGED DECKS: EASY TO AVOID, EXPENSIVE TO FIX

IRRIGATION SYSTEMS ARE A GREAT GARDEN MAINTENANCE TIME-SAVER

Irrigation is simple

Watering your garden can be as easy as getting out a hose and spraying some water over your plants whenever you think they might need a bit of a drink. And certainly many people enjoy watering their garden the old-fashioned way. They contemplate the world, pull a few weeds out of the lawn and talk to the dog as they nourish their garden.

Many people also incorporate some sort of irrigation system into their garden design. And if you're not talking about a huge area, it doesn't have to be at all fancy. An oscillating sprinkler will take care of a patch of turf, while black poly pipe can be used for drip irrigation to target your garden beds, with all sorts of connectors and precision drippers able to make them work for different configurations. If you run the tubing through your garden beds and attach it to your main water supply or a rainwater tank, you can turn your irrigation system on and off whenever needed.

A fairly inexpensive addition to your watering system is a battery-operated automated timer. You simply set the timer with the days and start times you'd like it to come on, along with the running time. It's a great option for people who are busy or spend periods of time travelling. You

only need to change the battery every 4–6 months and, unlike more complicated watering systems that plug into power and require valves, you can easily set this up yourself.

Finally, there are the solenoid systems powered by a control box that plugs into a power point, either in a garage or on an outdoor wall. These systems require no battery changes (although they do have batteries in case your power goes out for a period) and can also do more separate runs to all different garden beds all over your property. You can hook up rain sensors to them to ensure the watering system doesn't come on and waste water when it's raining. Many can now be controlled and changed via phone apps, so you can change the settings if you see a hotter forecast while you're away on holidays.

Have a chat to your landscaper about what watering system might work best and most efficiently for the garden you come up with together.

DIY SAVER: INSTALL A DRIP IRRIGATION SYSTEM

When it comes to watering garden beds, an above-ground drip irrigation system is great for both water and time efficiency. It will save you a lot of time watering your garden, and directs water to where it is needed, allowing the water to drip slowly and directly to the root zone of your plants for maximum absorption and minimal evaporation. And you don't need to be much of a handyperson to install one yourself.

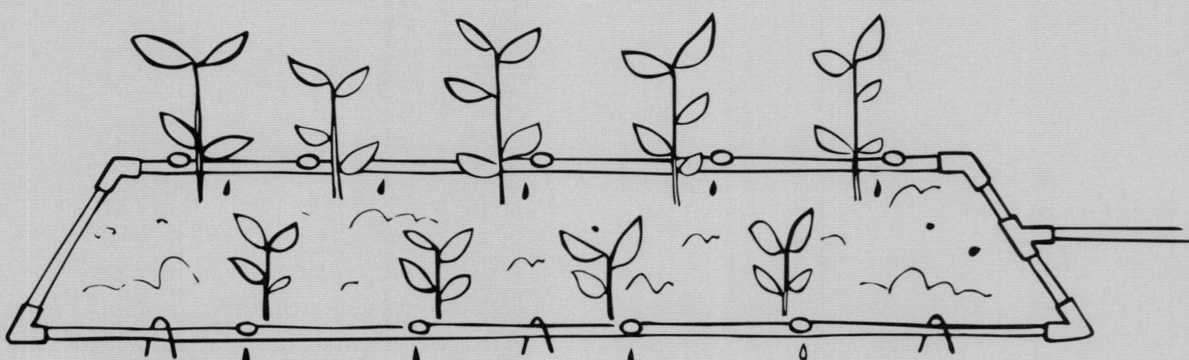

YOU WILL NEED

- » 13 mm or 19 mm black poly pipe; 20 metres is generally the smallest roll available
- » Sharp secateurs for cutting the piping
- » Irrigation pegs, sold in packs of 20, 50 or 100, depending on how many you'll need; usually 1 peg for every linear metre or so of poly pipe is enough to pin the tubing hard down to the ground so it doesn't become a trip hazard
- » Spike puncher to pierce the poly pipe so you can attach the dripper tubes
- » Dripper flexi tube, which comes in lengths of 5, 10 and 25 metres
- » Double-end adapters, which usually come attached with each dripper spike
- » One dripper for each plant (or it can be shared) – or if you're irrigating a whole garden section, it would be better to use a section of 13 millimetre dripper tubing, which is like poly pipe with inbuilt drippers every 20 centimetres or so
- » Snap-on connectors – straight ones, as well as 90-degree elbow connectors and/or T-shape connectors as required, so you can connect the poly pipe to a tap, and then run it to where it is needed in the garden. For example, 90-degree elbow connectors can get you around corners, while T-shape connectors can feed a new line of pipe while keeping the original line running
- » Locking clamps – one for every point at which the poly pipe slides onto a connector
- » End cap
- » Multi-grip pliers to tighten locking clamps

HOW TO DO IT

1. Roll out the poly pipe, then use secateurs to cut it to fit the length of garden you wish to irrigate. Pin the tubing down in place using irrigation pegs, spacing them every metre or so to keep the piping securely in place, so you won't be constantly tripping over it.

2. Using a spike puncher, insert a hole into the pipe behind each plant, making sure the hole is on the *side* of the pipe, facing towards the plant.

3. Cut a small piece of dripper tube for each of the holes you've punched. Make sure the dripper tube portions are the right length by holding them between the hole in the poly pipe and the plant before cutting.

4. Use double-end adapters to fix the dripper tubes to the pipe. Then put the drippers on the other end of the dripper tubes and place them next to the base of each plant.

5. Use connectors and locking clamps to join up the ends of the poly pipe. At the far end of your poly pipe – the one furthest from your tap – you'll need to add an end cap.

6. Now attach the whole system to the garden tap (or automated controller) using appropriate connectors, and use teflon tape on threads to prevent leaks. Turn it on to make sure everything works.

It's a good idea to allow water to flush through the entire line the first time you use it. Hook it up with the end plug removed, so that any dirt that may have entered the line during installation can be flushed out. This will stop the dirt getting stuck in the dripper heads and causing a blockage. Note that a pressure reducer will most likely need to be added at the tap for most low-pressure drip systems.

WHAT COULD GO WRONG?

All sorts of things! Inadequate drainage and poorly installed watering systems can create a waterlogged garden, in which many of your plants will suffer or die as a result of root rot.

On an even bigger scale, inadequate drainage can cause massive structural issues with your house and any other buildings on your property – as well as potentially affecting neighbouring properties.

Do it right the first time around and you'll avoid a lot of unnecessary heartache and expense further down the track.

CHAPTER 7

...

BUDGETING FOR LANDSCAPING

The best – and first! – thing to do when considering landscaping your property is to set a budget.

If a landscaper knows, from the beginning, exactly how much money they have to work with, they can be honest with you right from the start.

You may not have enough cash on hand to afford your absolute dream garden, but a landscaper can look at options you have to save money, and offer you suggestions as to how you can reduce your costs.

It is always much better for both parties to understand exactly what can be accomplished within the budget.

Think outside the square

A good landscaper should be able to offer a range of options to achieve the desired outcome for an outdoor space. Often this involves using some clever alternatives, so you can still get what you want without blowing out the budget. A lot of savings can be achieved by using alternative materials, such as compacted toppings instead of paved or concreted surfaces – which will also dramatically reduce labour costs to get the project completed.

WHICH BITS CAN *YOU* DO?

A blank canvas is always a good starting point for a landscaper to work with. If you are willing and able to do some work yourself – such as clearing the site of unwanted trees, vegetation, existing structures, edging, rocks, sleepers, paving or damaged concrete slabs – you'll save money. Even if you don't want to take on these tasks, and as long as any preliminary demolition and clearing required is not too full-on, it will be cheaper to hire some labourers to take on any manual work, as you don't need a qualified tradesman to undertake demolition or general labour.

BEWARE FALSE ECONOMY

In saying this, some clients ask to do jobs such as planting or lawn-laying themselves to save costs. However, if these tasks are done poorly due to lack of skill, it can actually cost more if your new plants or lawn suffer or need replacing as a result. Also, if you pay a reputable landscaper to do the work, they should, at least, guarantee the health of your new plants and lawn, and replace anything that dies within a period of 6–12 months. This isn't necessarily standard across the industry, but is good practice, so it's worthwhile checking your landscaper's policy in this regard.

Basically, only *you* know your true skills and capabilities, so don't take on tasks you're unsure about just to try to save money. Anything beyond your technical skills is always best left for a qualified landscaper or tradesperson to undertake, or you could end up with a lot of unforeseen costs when you have mistakes fixed by a professional.

Let's run through some of the general costs you'll incur when you are landscaping your garden.

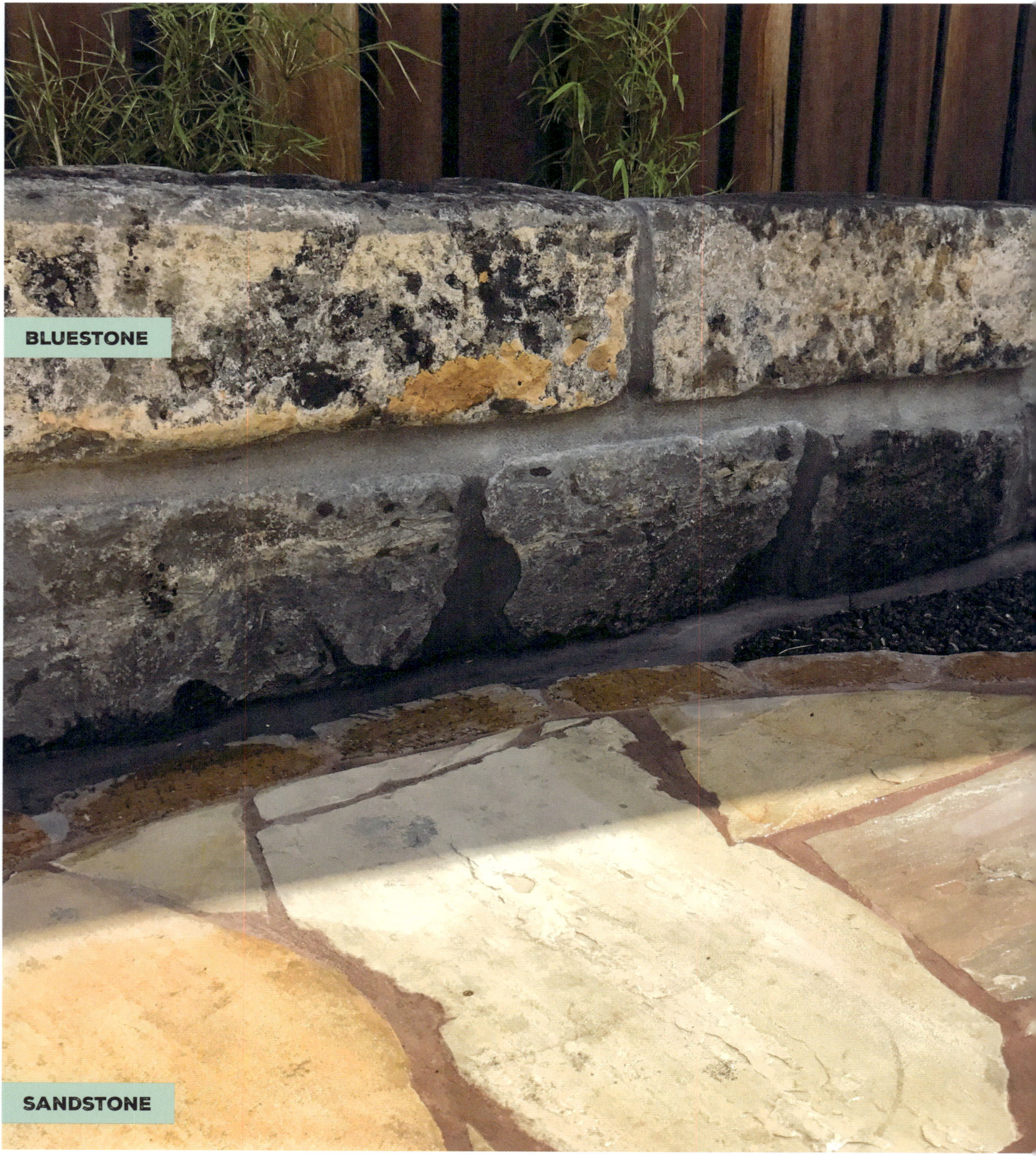
BLUESTONE
SANDSTONE

Incorporating hardscaping

A hardscaped area, such as a fire pit or outdoor dining area, is a popular request from homeowners during initial consultations. This is hardly surprising, given how often these feature in home and garden magazines and books, as well as on television design programs. People are consumers and love following trends.

As great as these areas look, though, most homeowners wouldn't use these spaces very frequently once construction has been completed. On the other hand, for the savvy renovator, these beautiful outdoor areas do appeal to potential buyers who want a ready-to-go entertainers' home, and such additions can definitely add more value to a property when it comes time to sell. For that reason, I would never say these feature areas are a waste of money – but they are indeed a luxury.

STONE: EXPENSIVE BUT SUBLIME

Natural stone hardscapes sit right at the top of the pricing list, and rightly so. These materials are naturally sourced, mined, and then cut to size, and contain a natural beauty that is impossible to recreate using concrete, plastic or any other material.

IRREGULARLY SHAPED PAVERS CREATE A NATURAL EFFECT

Stone paving, such as bluestone, sandstone or slate, when used in gardens and professionally installed by a landscaper, always looks magnificent, and the money spent is easily justified. For smaller areas, I would definitely recommend the extra expense of these materials compared to cheaper options such as concrete pavers. Across larger areas, however, the cost difference quickly adds up.

Similarly, as an easy way to create some wow factor, I would suggest using natural stone for a feature wall (whether dry stack or wet-lay) when retaining or separating outdoor areas, rather than a cheaper option such as timber sleepers with steel uprights. Again, this is a luxury element, so for the average homeowner, it is far easier to justify as an extra expense when it is used sparingly, or in a smaller area.

WHAT ABOUT PATHS AND DRIVEWAYS?

When it comes to traffic areas, consider what sort of traffic you'll be dealing with. Areas where there is only foot traffic might simply require a compacted topping as a finish, and perhaps a compacted crushed rock base as a subsurface. (For more on this, see pages 72–3.)

CONCRETE PAVERS ARE
A CHEAPER OPTION

SOME SIMPLE EDGING WILL STOP YOUR MULCH FROM SPILLING OUT ONTO THE DRIVEWAY

If cars and other vehicles will be using the area, you'll need a concrete subsurface or finished surface. Crushed-rock subsurfaces are much more cost-effective than concrete slabs. Compacted toppings or loose stone areas often reduce the need for surface drainage, since they – unlike concrete and paving – are permeable surfaces, which means rainwater can still penetrate through into the ground and drain away naturally. Paved or concrete surfaces can generate run-off or pooling of water, and they nearly always require the addition of a drain or drains – another extra cost.

For peace of mind, regardless of what the surface is, when it is close to a home's foundations, I always recommend incorporating at least an agricultural pipe (a flexible, corrugated drainage pipe with holes in it to collect water) connected to the stormwater drain.

For paths, compacted toppings with inset stone steppers don't cost nearly as much to install as full paving or concreting, yet still offer a desirable feature, so this is an option worth considering if you want the 'wow' without the big bucks.

Calculating the greenery

SMALL IS BEAUTIFUL...

Smaller plants, rather than mature ones, can save you money if you don't mind waiting for them to grow. In the long run, they'll be stronger, too, because they take root in the soil from a younger age, giving them a greater hold. With strong, deep roots, they're also less likely to get blown over in strong winds once they do reach maturity, and will be less reliant on watering as their deeper roots are able to extract more moisture from deep within the soil.

Just how much difference can purchasing smaller plants make to your budget? Here are some general price comparisons, just to give you an idea.

Let's say you can buy a crepe myrtle – a flowering Australian native that grows up to 7 metres tall – in a 20-centimetre pot for about $30; a more mature one in a 45-litre pot can cost up to $200. A small Meyer lemon tree might sell for about $13, while a bigger one might cost $45.

It doesn't require a mathematics degree to work out that if you're on a limited budget, it can be far more economical to buy smaller plants and trees and take good care of them in their early stages of life.

CREPE MYRTLE

LEMON TREE

BUT BIGGER IS QUICKER!

If your budget stretches a little further, it is a good design idea to buy some key mature plants – ones that can create shade or add a focal point in the garden – then fill the spaces in between with some fast-growing species that will eventually catch up. When you're planting mature trees, they will need to be staked for around two spring-growth periods to help support their height and weight after being planted until their new roots have grown and provide enough stability and strength. After that time, remember to remove the stakes, otherwise the trees can begin to depend on them for support rather than taking root properly themselves, which can cause stability problems later on.

PLANTING A BORDER

It's nice to replace harder materials in a landscape with softer ones wherever you can. As an example, you could remove a stone or concrete garden bed edge and use plants as a border instead. Thankfully, this is a relatively easy task, and the results will look great.

Want to try it out? I'd recommend digging a shallow trench along the edge of the garden bed's entire length to plant your border plants into. You'll want each plant spaced closely enough so that they're almost touching, to ensure a thick, instant border is created. If you choose foliage colour, textures and flowers carefully, and with a designer's eye, planted garden bed edges or path borders can create dramatic interest in no time at all.

Great choices for borders include common sage, mondo grass, flax lilies (*Dianella*), and species of ajuga, stachys and liriope. Your local garden design centre will be able to suggest other suitable alternatives for your garden area.

MONDO GRASS

LIRIOPE

STACHYS

Laying down the lawn

Instant turf is a fantastic product. It comes with a thickness of roots already attached to soil, so it will survive as long as it is watered and has a bedding of loam its roots can grow into. Best of all, it looks as though you have an established lawn on the same day it is laid out. Another benefit is that its carpet-like surface restricts weed growth. Instant turf is available in many species; these days you can expect to pay about $10–12 per square metre for most of them.

Laying down instant turf is a project that can be achieved by the keen DIY-er. If you've never done it before, you can google 'how to lay turf' and you'll come up with a number of simple, four-minute how-to online videos that will show you how to complete it properly.

The important first step is to ensure the area is prepared properly, which will make it easy to roll out the lawn. First, you need to make sure your ground levels are correct. You might think the ground needs to be completely level but, in fact, you need to ensure the ground falls away slightly from your house – this is essential for drainage reasons. You can adjust the levels using a shovel, rake and lawn leveller, and build them up using a bedding of sandy loam, at least 4 centimetres deep, which is also good for encouraging the lawn to take root.

Before you roll the turf out, sprinkle some lawn fertilising granules over the loam layer to aid the lawn's root growth. As soon as you have rolled out the turf, you should give it a good watering. Do not walk on it once it has been watered, or you'll end up leaving foot indents that will remain once the soil dries. Let your instant turf dry overnight, after which you can walk on it.

The other, cheaper option is to grow a lawn from seed, but you'll need to rope off the seeded area for a month or so, and it will require a lot of upkeep in terms or watering and weeding – especially weeding. People walking on the grass shoots before they are ready will also damage the lawn, plus it continues to be very susceptible to weed growth. Unwanted seeds are easily introduced through wind or via birds, and you'll need to keep pulling out young weeds so they don't take over.

Believe me, the extra money you spend on an instant lawn will be justified in the reduced hours of upkeep needed to ensure a seeded lawn remains weed-free during establishment.

COMMON LAWN SPECIES

KIKUYU BUFFALO COUCH ZOYSIA FESCUE

KIKUYU A grass with a medium-wide leaf and a soft-green colour, kikuyu thrives with full sun and heat. During winter months, it can fall dormant for about eight weeks.

BUFFALO This grass used to be scratchy and harsh, but newer varieties have a softer leaf. It is durable, resistant to weeds and is tolerant of shade.

COUCH This is a finely bladed grass that grows quickly and is resistant to drought. It is also hard wearing, but it does need to be mowed often.

ZOYSIA The blade of this grass is slightly wider than that of couch, and grows very densely. It is resistant to wear, tolerant of shade and doesn't need a lot of water.

FESCUE A good choice for cooler climates because it is frost-resistant. It has a fine blade and deep green colour, but it does require a lot of water.

WHAT ABOUT SYNTHETIC TURF?

Synthetic turf has come a long way since the first generation of AstroTurf, but many people are still reluctant to consider it for their backyards. These days, however, there are lots of different varieties that appear almost completely natural, thanks to subtle variations in the length, colour and width of the blades, as well as different blade thicknesses. There are even special types made to go around pools. From a distance, you can't tell that you're not looking at a lush lawn someone has spent many hours watering and mowing!

There are other benefits, too, apart from not having to do any watering, fertilising, weeding or mowing. Synthetic turfs don't wear down, aren't affected by extremes of weather, and are virtually indestructible when it comes to kids and pets. Most suppliers also offer a long warranty on strength and colour.

If you're thinking about the possibility of laying synthetic turf in the backyard, get some samples so that you can see how they feel, and put them in the sunshine to check what they look like in the environment in which they'll be installed.

The lowdown on decks and pergolas

When it comes to compromise during landscape design, it's mostly always decks and pergolas that lose out and end up smaller than a homeowner had originally envisaged.

People often tell me they want a backyard where they can entertain their friends and families, and they have it in their head they'll need a gigantic deck to do that. Good design, however, is as much about achieving a proportionally pleasing aesthetic as it is about creating a practical and usable space. So with this in mind, the biggest possible deck is not always the best design option – and most definitely not your best cost option.

TIMBER

Most people use real timber for decks and pergolas, which can cost around $200 per square metre for treated pine and upwards of $320 per square metre for hardwood. As the least expensive option, treated pine might seem like a good idea if you're on a budget, but you need to make sure it gets oiled or stained properly with a deck treatment product to ensure it lasts, as it won't be as hard-wearing or weather as well as a hardwood deck. Merbau is a

HARDWOOD DECK

relatively affordable and popular hardwood, often sourced from South-East Asia. Do make sure it has been harvested sustainably, as this isn't always the case.

In Australia, several native hardwoods are available. Some, like blackbutt, jarrah and spotted gum, are fire-resistant. Spotted gum warps and pops if nailed down, so it has to be screwed down, while blackbutt is susceptible to cracking if not sealed. Ironbark is probably the hardest and heaviest hardwood, which makes it more difficult to work with, but also means it is incredibly durable. It can cost in the realm of $450 per square metre.

Check with your landscaper or hardware store about other local or native timbers suitable for decking, and what their maintenance requirements would be.

Consider Composite Boards, Too

There is another option as well. If you're landscaping on a budget or live near the sea, check out composite decking. It is made from a combination of wood fibre, plastics and a binding agent to create a material that is stronger, denser and heavier than natural wood. From a maintenance point of view, a composite deck doesn't need seasonal oiling.

Composite decking boards have already evolved in the short time they have been on the market, which has definitely made them more appealing. Originally they were available only in a few colour options and about five grain patterns, which made it easy to see the same identical grain on boards laid close to one another, and therefore easy to spot that the boards were artificial. Now, composite boards are available in more colour options and up to 15 different grain variances, as well as in different widths and thicknesses, to create a more natural appearance.

Some other big ticks for composite decking boards are that they are made using recycled materials (mainly plastics) for their construction, they don't splinter or crack like real timber, and the boards can be ordered to whatever length you need: for a large deck you can order boards that span the entire width of the deck, which eliminates joins and creates a neat and tidy look. Depending on the brand you choose, composite decking can cost anywhere between $100 and $350 per square metre.

Don't forget, though, that if your decking is raised, you'll also need to factor in the cost of stairs and balustrading. The most cost-effective is a timber and wire balustrade, while glass balustrading – a popular choice if a deck has a great view – is the most expensive at about $320 per metre.

CHECK WITH YOUR COUNCIL

Before you even get started with designs for a deck or pergola, you need to visit your local council to see what, if any, restrictions exist. All of them will have regulations that cover issues like structural integrity, the materials that can be used in your area, minimum construction standards and boundary requirements (particularly for any structure with a roof).

Once you have these sorted out, you can take your council's list of regulations to your builder or landscaper so they can advise what will work best.

You'll then need to take the designs back in to your local council and get a planning approval and a permit. These do cost money – but not as much as having to pay a fine or tear the finished construction down, which is always a possibility. Even if that doesn't happen, if you ever sell your home and don't have legitimate paperwork for any added structures, savvy buyers will try to knock down the asking price to cover any possible costs to have permits produced retrospectively.

COMPOSITE DECKING

TIMBER & WIRE BALUSTRADE

GLASS BALUSTRADE

Capturing a precious resource: water!

Water tanks are a fantastic, sustainable addition to your outdoor area, and your plants and lawns will love soaking up pure rainwater during drier periods. With town water costs increasing all the time, why wouldn't you invest in some tanks and a pump so you can harness and use the rainwater that falls on your roof for free? Rainwater is also much 'softer' than water from the mains supply as it is free of the chemicals that are added to mains water to make it suitable for human consumption.

The beauty of modern rainwater systems is that if your rainwater tank runs dry, the pump running your watering system or hose will automatically switch back to using mains water. Whichever way you look at it, it makes good sense to harvest a natural resource that falls free from the sky in its purest form, rather than having your local council collect it and sell it back to you.

Even a smaller tank of 500–1000 litres will collect enough rainwater for a hobby gardener, and will sustain a vegie patch. If you don't have much space and a small budget, it is definitely worth considering. Anything is better than nothing, right?

If you have an extremely large roof area, or multiple roofs from which to collect rainwater, you can invest in a larger, connected, multiple tank set-up. This is where you can really start harnessing some savings, since you can use the excess stored rainwater for showering, doing the laundry, flushing toilets and other household needs. My mum always says her hair feels softer when she washes it with rainwater.

Much like solar panels, these fantastic sustainable investments initially cost a bit to purchase and install, but will repay you in spades well into the future. If you're planning to stay in your home for six or more years, they're a great idea.

And don't worry, you'll never have to deal with any problems caused by an overflowing tank, because once your tank is full, any excess water goes to stormwater from a connected overflow pipe.

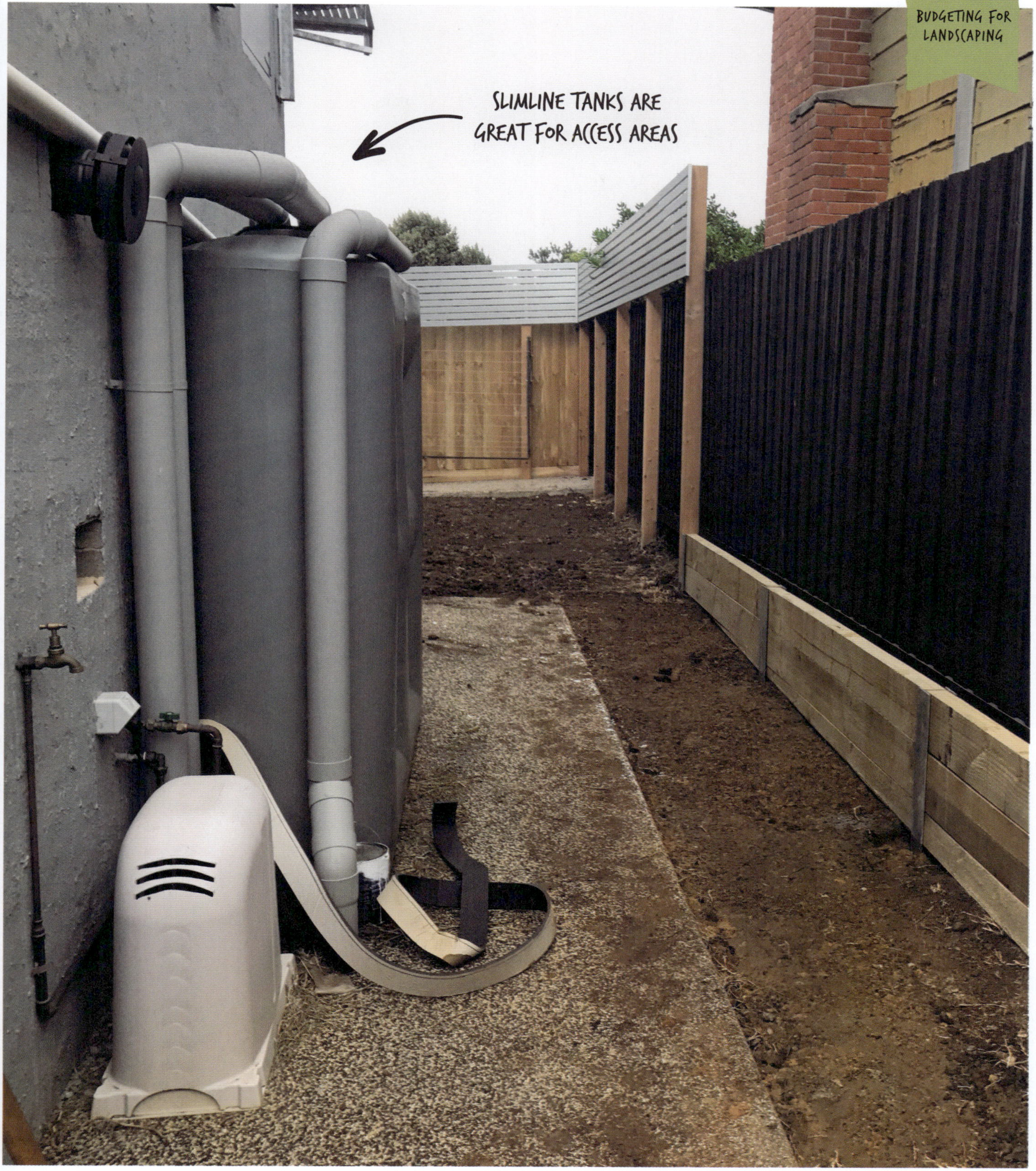
SLIMLINE TANKS ARE
GREAT FOR ACCESS AREAS

TYPES OF TANKS

There are plenty of different styles of tanks on the market. One type you'll remember if you've ever lived on a farm are the round, corrugated-iron tanks (these days also made of polyethylene) that come in a whole range of sizes. If you live on an acreage, they are a really cost-effective option, but they aren't very practical if you only have a small backyard space.

Much more popular for those living on a suburban block – or even in a townhouse with a courtyard area – are slimline poly tanks with a capacity of 2000–5000 litres that can be set up against a wall or fence. They will probably cost between $600 and $2200, a small pump and cover will cost about $500, and the extra fittings, like pipes and coupling, another $200. On top of that, make sure you factor in any delivery and installation costs.

If you're really squeezed for space, you could have an underground tank installed, particularly if you intend to live on the property for a number of years. Obviously, since there's earthmoving involved, and a load-bearing element has to be built over the tank for safety, underground tanks are far from the cheapest option.

BUDGETING HACKS

Once you've set your landscaping budget, it's easy to imagine all the things you could spend that money on and incorporate into your outdoor space.

What many clients forget to include in their dream designs, however, is the cost of labour – after all, you need someone to actually bring your ideas to life and create a beautiful space you can use. Be aware that labour costs can be considerable, eating up some 40–50 per cent of your budget – so to get a truer idea of what you'll *really* get for your money, it's more realistic to imagine spending only about half your entire budget on the design elements and the rest on labour.

When you've finalised your design, be sure to ask two or three different companies to provide you with a quote, so you can pick the one that suits you best. Remember, though, that the cheapest quote is not always the best. Check the fine print so you know exactly what is and *isn't* included in the price. The quality of the company's work should also be taken into account. Be sure to check out some of their previous projects – a good landscaper will usually be happy to provide some references, so you can talk to former clients and see the job they've done to get an idea of their attention to detail and quality of finishes.

A high quality of construction is definitely worth paying a little extra money for.

CAT
Ditch Witch
SK755

STAGE 1: LAYING THE FOUNDATIONS FOR LATER WORKS

Staging outdoor designs

A great financial option, especially for first homeowners, is to have your landscaping completed in stages, at perhaps 3–6 month intervals, so you don't have to outlay a big chunk of money all at once. Here's how to go about it.

STAGE 1

During this first block of work, consider what excavation needs to be carried out. You'll need to correct the soil levels across the yard and prepare a base for future construction work. This could involve concrete footings, compacted crushed-rock areas, bringing in quality loam or garden soils, and constructing retaining walls and drainage works. All of these jobs can be finished off to a neat, usable standard, where the yard can still be safely accessed until you are ready to embark on the next construction stage, when most of these surfaces will be covered.

STAGE 2

If not completed during Stage 1, now is the time to take care of hardscaping – paving, decking, concrete paths, driveways – as well as some softscaping, such as laying down turf and mulch, to keep weeds to a minimum until you're ready to proceed to the next stage.

STAGE 2: PAVING, DECKING,
ADDING TURF ...

STAGES 3 & 4: PLANTING, IRRIGATION AND FINISHING TOUCHES

STAGE 3

This is likely to include planting, which can be a fairly large expense, and possibly installing an automated watering system or garden lighting if there's still some leftover budget at this point.

STAGE 4

Now's the time to add any outdoor furnishings, such as tables, couches and barbecues, or extra construction features such as boxed seating, pergolas, water features, screens, pots and vertical gardens, or whatever else is needed to complete your project. Congratulations: you can now sit back and enjoy your wonderful garden!

WHAT COULD GO WRONG?

Doing lots of pre-planning will give you the best opportunity to have a beautiful garden, completed in good time and to your budget. The problem is that, with so many different elements involved, most people forget to factor something in when they're adding up the numbers. That's why it's so important to get a professional on board – even if you later decide to take on some of the work yourself.

When I'm working on a project, I cost in all these factors:

- Demolition and excavation
- Soil
- Plumbing (drains, pipes, watering systems)
- Turf
- Hard surfaces, from concrete to paving
- Structures, such as retaining walls, decking, balustrades, stairs, seating and screens
- Fencing
- Electricals for garden, deck and stair lighting, heating bars, fans and the like
- Plants
- Labour

If you've never taken on landscaping before, it will be all too easy to forget about one or more of these elements when doing your planning. Which ends in one of two ways: either you end up spending more money than you'd anticipated, or you have to leave out some elements and save up some more money to put them in later.

Having good advice from the start sets clear expectations about what you can achieve within your budget.

CHAPTER 8

CREATING A SCHEDULE

I've lost track of how many times I've arrived for an initial consultation at someone's property, only to explain to them how much more difficult the job will be because they didn't get me in earlier. Fences built, gates up, carports and garages completed – *you* might be happy, but you've created a minefield for your landscaper.

When you're building or renovating a house, landscaping is often the last thing you think about, but you do that at your own peril. Creating a beautiful garden often requires the use of machinery – having easy access for it makes a project that much easier, faster and cost-effective to complete.

While the other tradespeople are busy completing their jobs, there are plenty of things a landscaper can get done. Plus, if your landscaper can get on site before building works are completed, they can easily bring in any excavators or loads of materials, such as stone paving, tiling or timber for decks. Once access becomes more difficult, these jobs might need to be done by hand, driving up labour costs.

Plan well ahead

Consulting a landscaper early, finding out what big jobs need to be done and when (and being organised) makes it easier for everybody. It also reduces the risk of damaging completed work from other trades. For example, if you get your lovely exposed aggregate driveway poured before the landscapers have completed their work, chances are they might have to get materials delivered on it or drive machines over it, increasing the chance of chipping, cracking or staining – a scenario that could have been completely avoided.

Finished garages can block access, too. And it might not seem obvious, but even something like an installed hot water system can present a problem if it makes the only access path to the backyard too narrow to fit a wheelbarrow through. Now imagine how difficult that's going to make construction work. Plan ahead and all these kinds of issues can be prevented.

Walking through the steps

From my point of view, here's the ideal way to plan a garden: when you have the plans drawn up for your home (whether it's a new build or a renovation), ring your chosen landscaper. At your initial meeting, have your plans available, along with your scrapbook or Pinterest pages full of inspiration from chapter one. You'll also need a good idea of how much money you're able to allocate for all the outdoor

PLAN AHEAD SO EVERYTHING ARRIVES AT THE RIGHT TIME

PLANT LEGEND
Fruit or Citrus Tree
Existing Magnolia Tree
Flowering Shrub or Screening Bamboo
Carex Ornamental Sedge
Star Jasmine
Dichondra Silver falls
Synthetic Turf
Timber Posts with corrugated mesh attached for creeper to cover wall.
Compacted Topping
Garage
Retaining Wall
Re-used Bluestone Pitches as retaining wall.
Vegie Patch in Redgum
Bluestone step down
Rain Water Tank
RWT
Deck landing & stairs
Timber Balustrade
Bluestone or Basalt Round steppers.
Garden Shed
Existing Lawn
Existing Ornamental Pear

work. From all this information, we can tell how much room you have to work with, and whether your ideas are achievable given the budget and land footprint you have.

Then it's time to consider all the other factors that affect how we can construct your garden. For instance, we'll look at the aspect of your particular site, so we know how much sun different parts of your garden get and where prevailing winds might come from. The climate will play a huge part in how you should plan out your garden – do you want to create lots of shade or avoid it altogether to make the most of natural light?

Looking at the space you have, there'll be a lot to discuss: where can garden beds be put, is there space for a patch of lawn, what could your outdoor entertaining area look like, how much time will you need to spend in the garden to keep it looking beautiful, and what can be planted or built to offer privacy from the neighbours. This is also the time to discuss a pool, if you're considering one – the costs involved in putting it in, and whether it's even a good idea. You can also talk about whether you're imagining a native garden, one with beds for growing vegetables, or if you would like to create a tropical paradise.

Then there are all the practical considerations: the height and material used for fencing; where drainage and irrigation can be installed; what type of soil makes up the site (and whether you'll need to bring in truckloads of extra dirt to build up the land or make it suitable for cultivating trees and other plants); and where different parts of your intended design will work best.

ZOOMING IN ON A FOCAL POINT

One of the best ways to make an impact in a garden design, even in a small space, is by creating features that draw the eye. This could be as simple as choosing a beautiful tree, water feature, hedge, a statement pot, a sculpture or even a couple of brightly coloured chairs. It may depend on your budget as to what you choose as the garden's focus, but whatever it is, make sure it means something to you. There's really no point simply choosing a piece because you saw it in a magazine.

Think ahead, too. You might plant a fast-growing shade tree and place a bench below it where you can read a book. On the other hand, if you have little kids, a great sandpit or a raised bed where you can all grow tomatoes and other vegies might be your focal point.

Remember to think about scale. In a huge backyard, you might need a far more dramatic focus than if you're working within a small terrace or courtyard area.

Organising your time

Once you've worked on your plans and mapped out where you want everything to go, it will help if you work on a schedule that best overcomes some of the access issues mentioned earlier.

If you have a project manager working on the build, they can let you know when certain major construction events will take place. If you're doing that yourself, you'll need to keep on top of it so that you don't suddenly find you have to bring in a huge load of timber decking and have no way to get it into the backyard except through the house. Obviously, if you are fixing up the garden of a home that is already fully completed, you'll just have to make the best of whatever situation you find yourself in.

WHAT COULD GO WRONG?

They say timing is everything, and that's certainly the case when it comes to landscape constructions. Get it wrong and you put in place a whole load of potential problems. Imagine the extra expense of having to remove an already installed hot water system, or hiring extra labourers to cart heavy loads of soil, gravel or concrete through the house in a wheelbarrow. Cost isn't the only issue though. Imagine all the damage those big blokes in their boots could do to freshly finished wooden floors or newly laid carpets, or the chunks wheelbarrows can take out of walls.

Working out an excellent project plan – or having someone do that for you – can save a lot of time, money and hassle in the long run.

THANK YOU

Landscaping is a profession often taken up by like-minded people following a need to connect with the land and nature. I have been inspired by too many landscapers and landscape designers to mention, but there are always people to thank that personally helped encourage me to follow my passion.

TO THE MEDIA: To The Block (Julian Cress and David Barber) and Network 9, for giving me the opportunity to be on TV in front of an Australian audience enough to establish a public profile that led me to write this book. I doubt anyone would read a book by me without this sort of exposure.

TO HARDIE GRANT PUBLISHING: To all involved at Hardie Grant Publishing – without you, my words written on landscaping would still remain an unorganised mess resembling the ramblings of a madman. You've made the whole process not only achievable but also enjoyable through your great team members, so thank you.

TO MY REPRESENTATIVES: To Emma and Chris of BRAVO Management, thanks for finding me these often-unbelievable opportunities to do bucket list–type things such as writing a book. Have I told you I'd like to live in the Bahamas and star in a Hollywood blockbuster yet? We'll talk later, but the book thing is great, ta.

To Frank Lonergan: To my grandpa Frank – as a child I remember following you around your garden with the hose early in the morning, making sure the plants got a good drink before a hot day, and again at the end of one. I remember potting on some special ones you took clippings of out on a walk, or just plucking those pesky weeds. You gave me my first bonsai at age seven, and thirty years later I still have plenty. Your passion for gardening and plants obviously rubbed off and I hope to pass that on to my children and theirs in years to come.

To my past employers: Thanks to everyone who has employed me over the years and let me hone my skills in all the different aspects of this trade.

To tradespeople, labourers and suppliers: Part of the fun of practising a trade is the connections I make with other trades I need on a project, labourers I hire and the suppliers I talk to daily. The banter is always appreciated and definitely helps boost the mood through those winter months outside.

To my family: To Mum and Dad, Biddy and Pete, for always being supportive and encouraging and taking us camping every Easter, which is where I really fell in love with nature and our country. You both are some of the hardest workers I've ever met, which has no doubt instilled the great work ethic I take pride in having myself. To my sister, Laura, thanks for being tops, I may have forgotten you in my wedding speech years ago, but at least you're mentioned in this book! Surely that's some consolation and anyway, you've never mentioned me in any of the books you haven't written ...

To my wife, Sophie: For all your support with my work and away from it. You've always designed my business cards, with the first lot being the most ambitious, as we enclosed flower seeds in each one like a business card–sized seed pack. We may have simplified the cards since then, but your willingness to help me stand out will always make you the stand-out in my eyes. Although you may not love crazy paving (which makes me think you may be crazy), I love you like crazy ... pave.

And finally, to my newest and greatest inspiration, my kids, Van, Shepherd and Dulcie. You three make my world go round, and as yours does, I promise to forever fill it with plants and nature. Vine and Sons and Daughter is a mouthful for a business name, but I will register it now anyway just in case.

INDEX

E

F

G

H

I

J

K

L

T

V

W

Y

Z

Published in 2019 by Hardie Grant Books, an imprint of Hardie Grant Publishing

Hardie Grant Books (Melbourne)
Building 1, 658 Church Street
Richmond, Victoria 3121

Hardie Grant Books (London)
5th & 6th Floors
52–54 Southwark Street
London SE1 1UN

hardiegrantbooks.com

All rights reserved. No part of this publication may be reproduced, stored in a retrieval system or transmitted in any form by any means, electronic, mechanical, photocopying, recording or otherwise, without the prior written permission of the publishers and copyright holders.

The moral rights of the author have been asserted.

Copyright text ©Dale Vine 2019
Copyright photography: 20 (bottom), 36 (bottom left), 53, 64 (top), 65 (middle), 71 (bottom left), 74 (top), 131, 139, 151 (bottom), 155 (bottom), 168, 170 (top), 172, 173 (right), 178 (top), 188, 195, 199, 201 (bottom), 203 (left), 210 ©Dale Vine 2019; cover, 6, 9, 13, 39, 88, 110, 130, 157, 167 (top), 214, 218, author image on back cover flap ©Gavin Green 2019; **iStock**: 12, 26, 109 (bottom), 211 ©xavierarnau; 14 (top left), 140–141 ©cjp; 14 (bottom left) ©Chayantorn; 14 (bottom right) ©Estherrr; 17, 97 (top) ©Tom Merton; 18, 27 (left), 111, 162–163, 209 (top) ©KatarzynaBialasiewicz; 20 (top), 45 (bottom right) ©Available Light; 21, 42 ©Marilyn Nieves; 22 (top) ©Selena Gardner-Morrison; 22 (bottom) ©JohnnyGreig; 24, 32, 95, 108 (top) ©monkeybusinessimages; 25 (top) ©Paul Bradbury; 25 (bottom left) ©YinYang; 25 (bottom right), 93 (top) ©mrod; 27 (right) ©ElenaMorgan; 28 (left) ©ShutterWorx; 28 (right) ©HannamariaH; 29 (left), 60 (top), 96 ©jodie johnson; 29 (right), 73 (bottom right) ©oversnap; 30–31 ©Drbouz; 35 ©Mkovalevskaya; 36 (top) ©btplaczek; 36 (bottom right) ©Adam Calaitzis; 40–41 ©Chalabaia; 43 ©Kolbz; 45 (top) ©katkov; 45 (bottom left) ©gdmoonkiller; 48–49, 119 ©AleksandarNakic; 50–51 ©Irina88w; 54 (top) ©Nustock; 54 (bottom left) ©Anagramm; 54 (bottom right) ©boblin; 56–57 ©jnnault; 59, 61 (bottom), 98 (bottom) ©zstockphotos; 60 (bottom) ©pamspix; 61 (top) ©Wavebreakmedia; 64 (bottom left) ©c11yg; 64 (bottom middle) ©ooyoo; 64 (bottom right) ©SharonWills; 65 (top) ©HIT1912; 65 (bottom) ©Connie Kerr; 70 ©CBCK-Christine; 71 (top) ©VvoeVale; 71 (bottom right) ©Andrew Waugh; 73 (top left) ©simazoran; 73 (top right) ©andreygonchar; 73 (bottom left) ©ImageGap; 74 (bottom) ©sjwhite711; 75 (top) ©Stephen Barnes; 75 (bottom) ©ozgurcoskun; 76 (top left) ©Shalith; 76 (top right) ©tacojim; 76 (bottom) ©dpproductions; 77 ©vgajic; 78–79 ©jacquesvandinteren; 80 (top) ©thegoodphoto, 80 (bottom) ©Image Source; 81 (top) ©MNStudio; 81 (bottom), 146–147 ©Schulzie; 84–85 ©Peopleimages; 86 ©miller3181; 87 (top left) ©fasphotographic; 87 (top right) ©SbytovaMN; 87 (bottom) ©Anchly; 90 ©spyderskidoo; 91 ©brollymedia; 92 (top) ©CreativNature_NL; 92 (bottom left) ©SteveLuker; 92 (bottom right) ©Susan_Stewart; 94 ©caughtinthe; 97 (bottom) ©mbolina; 98 (top) ©AzmanL; 100 ©cmspic; 101 (top) ©Linda Raymond; 101 (bottom) ©wanderluster; 102 ©1mgorthand; 104–105 ©tripelem; 106–107 ©penguenstok; 108 (middle) ©ep_stock; 108 (bottom) ©yacobchuk; 109 (top) ©photovideostock; 114 (top left) ©Tony Feder; 114 (top right) ©saraTM; 114 (middle) ©mrberry; 114 (bottom left), 152 ©LazingBee; 114 (bottom right) ©bgwalker; 115 (top) ©trigga; 115 (bottom) ©JudieParkinson; 121, 136 (top) ©yellowsarah; 122 ©Eirasophie; 123 ©Tuangtong; 124–125 ©ploresempre; 126 ©tirc83; 127 (top) ©Adam Jeffers; 127 (bottom) ©therry; 129 (top) ©andrewgonchar; 129 (bottom left) ©stocker; 129 (bottom right) ©stocknroll; 136 (bottom) ©wayra; 137 ©AnnaGreen; 138 (top left) ©TommyIX; 138 (top right), 183 ©Supersmario; 138 (middle right) ©nerudol; 138 (bottom left) ©PeterMulaj; 138 (bottom right) ©Alexh; 142 ©AndreaObzerova; 143 ©JasonJiron; 144–145 ©DGLimages; 149 ©Marccophoto; 150 ©kerkia; 151 (top) ©CarrieCaptured; 151 (middle) ©Jack Mullins; 153 (top) ©Bruceman; 153 (bottom) ©Joe_Potato; 154 ©Maybaybutter; 155 (top) ©Paul Maguire; 156 ©MarcoMarchi; 161 ©Georgina198; 164–165 ©frazac; 167 (bottom) ©mikkelwilliam; 173 (left) ©Martin Wahlborg; 174 (top) ©Robire; 174 (bottom) ©AnikaSalsera; 175 ©Pattanaphong Khuankaew; 176 ©eyjafjallajokull; 177 ©lolostock; 178 (middle) ©Bohee Hyun; 178 (bottom) ©valery_green; 179 ©BrettCharlton; 180 ©Jamie Haxby; 184 ©PongsakornJun; 187, 212–213 ©Delpixart; 189 ©Kiwimate; 191 (left) ©JustinSmith; 191 (top right) ©chuckcollier; 191 (bottom right) ©jnnault; 192 ©sarahdoow; 194, 200 (middle) ©Willowpix; 200 (top) ©jonathansloane; 200 (bottom) ©BanksPhotos; 201 (top left) ©BrilliantEye; 201 (top right) ©shank_all; 202 (top) ©ozgurdonmaz; 202 (bottom left) ©tenmuzcan; 202 (bottom right) ©gpointstudio; 203 (top right) ©Eirasophie; 203 (bottom right) ©ehaurylik; 204–205 ©ChristianChan; 206–207 ©yunava1; 209 (bottom) ©CarolSvec; 215 ©Rawpixel; 216–217 ©Dougberry; **Shutterstock**: 14 (top right) ©Marie Linner; 93 (bottom) ©metalstock; 118 ©BondRocketImages; 196 ©zstock; **Stocksy**: 44, 171 ©Trinette Reed; 63 ©Gillian Vann; 82–83, 170 (bottom) ©Rowena Naylor; **Unsplash**: 1–2 ©Nagesh Badu; 10–11 ©Nick Morrison; 138 (middle left) ©Markus Spiske
Copyright illustrations ©Sinéad Murphy 2019
Copyright design ©Hardie Grant Publishing 2019

NATIONAL LIBRARY OF AUSTRALIA

A catalogue record for this book is available from the National Library of Australia

Dale Vine's Outdoor Reno Guide
ISBN 978 1 74379 5132

10 9 8 7 6 5 4 3 2

Publishing Director: Pam Brewster
Managing Editor: Marg Bowman
Project Editor: Anna Collett
Editor: Katri Hilden
Design Manager: Jessica Lowe
Designer/Illustrator: Sinéad Murphy
Production Manager: Todd Rechner
Production Coordinator: Mietta Yans

Colour reproduction by Splitting Image Colour Studio

Printed in China by Leo Paper Product. LTD.